Historic Pubs & Inns of WARWICKSHIRE

DAVID HANCOCK

COUNTRYSIDE BOOKS
NEWBURY, BERKSHIRE

First Published 1995
© David Hancock 1995

COUNTRYSIDE BOOKS
3 Catherine Road
Newbury, Berkshire

ISBN 1 85306 369 X

Cover illustration by Syrah Arnold
Photographs by Bonita Toms
Map by Trevor Yorke

Produced through MRM Associates Ltd., Reading
Typeset by Paragon Typesetters, Queensferry, Clwyd
Printed in England by Woolnough Bookbinding, Irthlingborough

Contents

Coleshill ②   ① Shustoke

Withybrook ③

Hampton -In-Arden ⑤   ④ Monks Kirby

Berkswell ⑦   Easenhall ⑥

Barston ⑧

⑨ KENILWORTH

⑩ Five Ways

Lowsonford ⑪

Henley In Arden ⑫   WARWICK ⑬ ⑭

⑮ Wootton Wawen

Napton-on -the-Hill ⑰

Southam ⑯

Aston Canhow ⑱

Harbury ⑲   Priors Marston ⑳ ㉑

⑫ Alveston

Temple Grafton ㉔

Gaydon ㉕   Priors Hardwick ㉓

STRATFORD UPON AVON ㉖ ㉗ ㉘

Broom ㉙

Alderminster ㉚

Edgehill ㉛   ㉝ Warmington

Whatcote ㉞   Ratley ㉜

Ilmington ㉟

Shipston on Stour ㊱

㊲ Lower Brailes

Great Wolford ㊳   ㊴ Long Compton

Little Compton ㊵

Introduction

Warwickshire, that most rural of English counties, is renowned for its lush green countryside, its network of meandering canals, and most of all, as the birthplace of the world's greatest playwright and poet, William Shakespeare.

Shakespeare's county is rich in history. Due to its central position in England, Warwickshire has long been a 'passing through' county, with people, notably marching armies, heading to distant areas. Two great armies met here at the Battle of Edgehill during the Civil War in 1642. Old droving routes and coaching turnpikes criss-crossed the area, linking London with the Midlands. Its close proximity to the mighty industrialised Midlands had a significant effect, with the construction of an intricate canal system that transported goods south to Oxford and London.

An interesting way to understand Warwickshire's development and bygone times is to delve into the history of its villages, especially the centuries-old pubs and inns. In my quest to find historic hostelries, I travelled all over the county seeking out ancient droving taverns, character coaching inns and attractively-sited canalside pubs. I discovered buildings of great antiquity as well as alehouses and village locals with a story or two to tell, such as tales of highwaymen, ghosts, Civil War connections and those supposedly visited by, or associated with, William Shakespeare. Also taken into consideration when selecting my forty inns were location, old-world charm, an acceptable quality of food and intimate links with village history. I have taken the historic boundaries of Warwickshire, incorporating some fine pubs between Coventry and Birmingham, and I have tried to achieve an even distribution of pubs across the county.

This book is more than just a 'historic guide'. Each pub is brought up-to-date, with details of interior comfort, character, atmosphere and dining ambience. The real ales are listed and notable selections of wines and whiskies are mentioned. Emphasis is placed on the style of food on offer and examples of dishes and specialities on both bar and restaurant menus are highlighted to whet your appetite.

Also featured are alfresco facilities—gardens, terraces—for eating and drinking. Children are now generally welcome in most pubs, but if there are any restrictions, such as they are only allowed in if eating, I have indicated the fact. Mention is also made as to the existence of a family room in the pub, or a children's play area in the garden. If an inn provides overnight accommodation, brief details are given as to the number of rooms and whether there are ensuite facilities.

An extra dimension to this guide is the inclusion of a 'Places of interest nearby' section. If you are planning a day out, incorporating a lunchtime or evening visit to the pub, this short list of museums, country parks, stately homes and attractive villages, should aid your research. Check with the nearest Tourist Information Centre for further information.

I have listed the opening hours and bar food times of each pub, as they can vary significantly, depending on the wishes of the landlord. Busy town pubs may be open all day Mondays to Saturdays, others only on market days and Saturdays. Rural pubs may close Sunday evenings and all day Mondays and have later opening times during the week. Standard Sunday hours are at present 12 noon to 3 pm (2.30 pm in some cases) and 7 pm to 10.30 pm. However, recent Government proposals now allow all-day opening on Sundays, although this is at the discretion of the landlord.

It is important to note that changes are inevitable. Landlords and chefs change frequently, leading to new menus and styles of cooking, different opening hours and bar food times and varying policies regarding children. Some pubs may even close altogether.

In researching and collating the information on the pubs included in this guide, I wish to thank all the landlords for their enthusiasm and assistance, Kevin Edwards for his expert 'local' knowledge of Warwickshire pubs, the staff at the Warwickshire County Record Office in Warwick for their help and my friend and colleague Bonita Toms who took the photographs and made invaluable notes in each pub.

I hope you will gain an insight into the history and charm of this unspoilt county by exploring the delights of these ancient inns and villages in which they stand. I certainly did.

David Hancock
Summer 1995

Shustoke
The Griffin Inn

1

Shustoke comprises two hamlets located a mile apart along the B4114. Church End, the smaller of the two, occupies high ground with good views across agricultural land and Whiteacre reservoir. It is by far the older settlement and contains romantic stone-and-brick buildings, the timber-framed Priory Farmhouse and Old Rectory and St Cuthbert's church, which was rebuilt in the late 19th century after a flash of lightning almost destroyed the original building, which had been in existence for some 500 years. Inside the church is a monument to Sir William Dugdale (1605-86), the great historian and antiquary who wrote the *Antiquities of Warwickshire* in 1656, and his tomb. He was born at the former rectory in Shawbury Lane.

On the sharp bend near the junction of Shawbury Lane and the B4114 can be found the Griffin Inn, which occupies a 200 year old brick building. However, on closer inspection it is clearly evident from the beamed interior that the brick façade encases an earlier timber-framed structure. Before modernisation the first floor area of the inn comprised two huge, timber-ceilinged rooms.

The Griffin sign is taken from the coat-of-arms of the Dugdales, who still own nearby Blythe Hall, and up until eleven years ago the Griffin was part of the large Dugdale estate. In 1888 the pub was both a farm and alehouse and run by William Auscott, who unfortunately fell down the cellar and broke his neck in 1905. By the 1930s the landlord of the Griffin was one Fletcher Fox, who doubled as the local undertaker, making coffins in the barn adjacent to the pub, most of which probably ended up in the churchyard opposite!

Today the outbuilding houses one of only two micro-breweries in Warwickshire, known as the Church End Brewery, the other being Judges Brewery in Church Lawford, near Rugby. The pub has for years attracted discerning real ale drinkers, but the addition of brews such as Gravediggers Ale, Vicars Ruin and Pews Porter to the extensive menu of beers, is now drawing ale fanatics from far and wide. The changing selection of eight beers may also include Theakston Old Peculier, Moorhouse's Pendle Witches Brew and Marston's Pedigree, all dispensed from beneath a heavy-beamed servery, as are the various farm ciders.

In recent years, the building has been sympathetically extended to cope with the increased popularity and the three comfortable, inter-connecting bars feature a wealth of beams, open log fires in winter and cushioned wall benches and settles. Pine tables and chairs and green garden furniture fill the conservatory, which makes the most of the countryside views. Outside, to the rear, there is a terrace.

The lunchtime bar menu lists sound pub snacks, such as mixed grill, lasagne, steak in ale, chilli and beef rogan josh, as well as a choice of salads and sandwiches. The specials board may offer, for example, lamb roast dinner, Chinese turkey steak and cod and chips.

Children are welcome in the conservatory, but not in the bar.

Opening hours: 12 noon to 3 pm and 7 pm to 11 pm. Bar food is available from 12 noon to 2.30 pm (but not on Sundays).

Telephone: 01675 481205.

How to get there: Shustoke is situated on the B4114 between Coleshill and Nuneaton, 3 miles north-east of Coleshill. There is a large car park to the side of the pub.

Places of interest nearby: Kingsbury Water Park and Visitor Centre, Kingsbury. Middleton Hall and Ash End House Farm ('The Children's Farm'), Middleton.

Coleshill
The Swan Hotel

2

As its name implies, this old market town stands on a steep hill above the river Cole, which is crossed by a fine medieval bridge. It is a place of great antiquity, dating back to Saxon times, and was a royal manor during the Norman period. Lords of the manor since the 16th century have been the Digby family, some of whom were involved in the Gunpowder Plot conspiracy. Sir Everard Digby was executed for his part in this and tradition has it that the idea was hatched at a meeting held in Coleshill Hall.

Dominating the centre of the town is the church of St Peter, with its magnificent steeple, rare Norman font and elaborate tombs of the Digby family. Nearby, on Church Hill, stand the village stocks, which are unique in the county as they combine a pillory and a whipping post.

Coleshill's heyday was the coaching era, when the then village was on the main London to Holyhead route. Mail was dropped here for Birmingham and horses changed at one of the 20 hostelries that lined the long main street. The largest of these coaching inns was the Swan, which today is a fine, listed, 17th-century building with a splendid overhanging cornice. Until quite recently it had an arched central carriageway leading to what were the stables at the rear. Addison, the one-time writer and essayist of *The Spectator* often stayed at the inn.

Major building work and renovations over recent years have resulted in a rear extension block of bedrooms. The Swan now has a total of 32 en suite rooms which are popular with travelling businessmen as the inn is only a mile from the M6 and the National Exhibition Centre is nearby. The central gravel track no longer exists – now it forms the entrance hall and reception area, with the Maxstoke and York bars and the restaurant leading from it. Everywhere is comfortably furnished and adorned with plenty of prints, lamps, shelves with pots, jugs, plates and books, plus cased shooting and fishing equipment. The Maxstoke bar houses the games and food servery.

The Swan belongs to Ansells brewery's small hotel group and offers their Best Bitter and Mild, as well as Tetley Bitter and Burton Ale on draught. In the bar the straightforward pub menu features filled jacket potatoes and baguettes, burgers, steak and kidney pie, scampi and lasagne. Specials may include tomato and basil pasta, lamb hotpot with pickled red cabbage and chilli with rice. More elaborate fare – for example prawn and monkfish creole, pork Stroganoff and rack of lamb – can be ordered from the restaurant menu. Traditional roast lunches are available on Sundays. Children are always made very welcome.

Opening hours: 11 am to 11 pm, with bar food served all day to 9.30 pm.

Telephone: 01675 464107.

How to get there: Coleshill is situated off the A446 east of Birmingham and is 1 mile from the M6, junction 4. There is a large rear car park.

Places of interest nearby: Kingsbury Water Park, Middleton Hall and a children's farm at Ash End House Farm, Middleton, all a few miles to the north.

Withybrook
The Pheasant

3

Withybrook is a pleasing collection of 17th to 19th-century half-timbered and brick cottages and more modern dwellings, nestling beside a picturesque brook amid peaceful, undulating countryside. The village was once known as Willowbrook, its name originating from the large number of willow trees that used to grow beside the water. These in turn produced withies which are used for thatching and eventually the settlement became 'Withybrook'. The parish incorporates one of Warwickshire's 'lost' villages. Recorded in the Domesday Survey, Hopsford depopulated in the early 17th century, but traces of this larger settlement can be seen in the fields to the west and north of Old Hall Farm.

Situated a stroll away from the charmingly positioned 14th-century church of All Saints, and making the most of its brookside setting, is the Pheasant, a popular 17th-century freehouse. Little is known about the early history of the building, but old photographs and records show that it was once called the Half Moon and was certainly the hub of the community. Local residents could buy fuel from a roadside petrol pump in front of the pub and purchase pork from one of the rear outhouses, where the publican also slaughtered pigs for his living.

The building has been opened up and extended in recent years, but the spacious front room still retains considerable character, with the presence of some polished flagstones, heavy beams, a few standing timbers and a low ceiling. The central brick fireplace and the assortment of rural implements decorating the walls add to the atmosphere in this friendly and efficiently run establishment. Further seating is available in a connecting rear room and an adjacent smaller side bar.

Courage Directors, John Smith's Bitter and Scrumpy Jack cider are on handpump, and the well-stocked bar also offers an interesting short, global list of wines, many available by the half bottle.

A big attraction here is the selection of generously-served bar food on offer. The varied and extensive printed menu lists fisherman's pie, braised pheasant with mushrooms in a Madeira sauce, venison pie, steak and kidney pie, fresh fish dishes, various steaks and omelettes, plus well-filled rolls and sandwiches. Blackboard specials may highlight, for example, sizzling skillets – teriyaki beef and prawn Cantonese – grilled haddock, cod and salmon and Cajun-style chicken. There are also tempting vegetarian meals such as lentil and mushroom au gratin and vegetarian goulash. Sunday roasts are a feature.

The place to be on warm sunny days is on the gravelly brookside terrace where benches and brollies provide a splendid spot for an al fresco lunch. Children are allowed in the pub.

Opening hours: 11 am to 2.30 pm and 6.30 pm to 11 pm. Bar food is served from 12 noon to 2 pm and 6.30 pm (7 pm on Sundays) to 10 pm.

Telephone: 01455 220480.

How to get there: Withybrook is situated on the B4112 between Nuneaton and Rugby, 4 miles from the M6, junction 2. Limited parking is available at the rear of the pub.

Places of interest nearby: Lutterworth Museum to the east, H M Prison Services Museum at Newbold Revel College, to the south and Coombe Abbey Country Park at Binley, on the outskirts of Coventry.

Monks Kirby
The Bell Inn

The magnificent, soaring red sandstone tower of St Edith's church in this peaceful parish dominates the rich, undulating countryside that exists between Rugby and Nuneaton. A settlement has existed here since Saxon times, when Ethelfleda, daughter of King Alfred the Great, built the first church on the mound in the village in AD 917.

After the Norman Conquest, in 1077, King William of Normandy awarded a French knight, William de la Guerche, some land for his support during the campaign. He rebuilt the church and established a Benedictine priory nearby, endowing it with a prior and seven monks from an abbey in Angers. Cyricbrig, as the village was recorded in the Domesday Book in 1086, later became known as Monks Kirby due to the presence of the priory.

The present impressive church was built in the 14th century and extended a century later, incorporating the remains of the priory. During these early years, Monks Kirby was of a considerable size and importance, eventually achieving the status of a market town and welcoming many merchants and pilgrims. The church boasts some fine monuments of the Fieldings, Earls of Denbigh, who resided at nearby Newnham Paddox House until it was demolished in 1952. Only the splendidly decorated gates survive.

Situated at the end of Bell Lane, adjacent to an old track, is the Bell Inn, which has historic connections with the church and priory. A building has existed on the site since the 11th century, when it was used as a gatehouse from where the priory bells were rung. Over the centuries it became a brewhouse cottage and finally an inn.

The age of the present building is not known, but extensive renovation and extension in 1970 completely transformed the inn's appearance, disguising the historic heart of the pub. Timbers used to restore the building were obtained from a house at Lutterworth where John Wycliffe translated the Bible into English. The central bar of the pub is old, featuring a fine slabbed and cobbled floor, wall and ceiling beams and a cosy ambience. More recent additional rooms radiate off the main bar and blend in well with the ancient core.

The vast and varied printed menu specialises in Spanish food, notably using a wide range of fresh fish. Featured dishes include paella Valencia, halibut malengena, fish soup, rapé (monkfish cooked in tomatoes, clams, mussels and white wine), chorizo al vino and Spanish chicken casserole. The menu also spans more conventional English pub food, such as various steaks, saddle of lamb and beef Wellington. Roasts are regularly available on Sundays.

Behind the bar one will find Boddingtons Bitter, Flowers Original and a guest brew, a list of 130 wines favouring interesting Spanish labels, plus a fine display of malt whiskies and rare vintage ports.

Outside there is a peaceful and sunny side terrace overlooking a small stream and open fields. Children are made very welcome both inside and out.

Opening hours: 12 noon to 3 pm and 6.30 pm to 11 pm. Bar food is served from 12 noon to 2.30 pm and 7 pm to 10 pm.

Telephone: 01788 832352.

How to get there: Monks Kirby is signposted off the B4112 between Rugby and Nuneaton. There is plenty of parking to the front of the inn.

Places of interest nearby: The James Gilbert Rugby Football Museum, in Rugby and Newbold Quarry Park, off the B4112 into the town. Lutterworth Museum is to the north-east of Monks Kirby and H M Prison Services Museum is to the south, at Newbold Revel College near Easenhall.

⑤ Hampton-in-Arden
The White Lion

Situated in pleasant, wooded countryside by the river Blythe, which is spanned by a packhorse bridge thought to be 500 years old, one of the few of these bridges left in the Midlands, this historic village was the traditional centre of the Forest of Arden, the setting for Shakespeare's *As You Like It*. Little now remains of the forest, but the cluster of old cottages and the 16th-century timber-framed Moat House that together surround the hilltop church, still survive and form the ancient nucleus to this now extensive settlement. It is, these days, primarily a dormitory village for both Birmingham and Coventry.

According to the Domesday Survey in 1086, an inn was even then opposite the church in the village, but it is not known whether it was on the site of the present-day hostelry, the attractive, white painted White Lion, which proudly stands opposite the wide lychgate. The present building, which unfortunately conceals its timber-framing, is thought to date back 600 years, when it is believed to have been a farmhouse. It is also said that nailmakers once used the building for their craft. Records confirm that it has been an inn for the past 150 years, with a succession of landlords during that time. Until relatively recently, the small, single-storey side extension was used as a sweet shop.

Step inside the White Lion and you will, surprisingly, find a very unpretentious interior. The carpeted lounge bar is homely and comfortable, with cushioned stools, wall bench seating and a sought-after window seat overlooking the churchyard. It is simply decorated with a few prints, brasses and some old copper lamps on the brick fireplace. The tiny public bar, Daniel's Bar, is a real gem. Totally unspoilt and a classic locals' drinking place, it features a red-tiled floor and red and cream painted brick walls beneath a low, beamed ceiling, and a vast inglenook with a small fireplace and wooden wall benches inside. The rear extension houses the dining room.

Mitchells and Butlers brewery, part of the Bass conglomerate, owns the pub, and you will find Brew XI, draught Bass and a guest brew on handpump. There is also a simple, yet varied, list of 27 wines. The standard bar menu offers home-cooked pub favourites, like steak and kidney pie, curry, lasagne and barbecue platter, with the specials board highlighting fresh cod in batter, minted lamb stir-fry and cauliflower and mushroom bake. The evening restaurant is renowned for its steaks, as well as dishes like rack of lamb and lemon chicken.

To the rear is a grass area with benches and those wishing to explore the area further can stay overnight in one of the seven en suite bedrooms. Children are warmly welcomed in the pub.

Opening hours: 12 noon to 11 pm. Bar food is served from 12 noon to 2 pm and 7 pm to 10 pm, and the restaurant is open in the evenings. No food is available on Sundays.

Telephone: 01675 442833.

How to get there: Hampton-in-Arden is situated on the B4102 between Solihull and Meriden. Adequate parking can be found to the rear of the pub.

Places of interest nearby: The National Exhibition Centre is 1 mile to the north, near junction 6 of the M42. Solihull, to the south-west is the home of the National Motorcycle Museum.

6 Easenhall
The Golden Lion Inn

Easenhall is a pretty little village tucked away in rolling countryside in the north-eastern corner of Warwickshire, between the bustle of Rugby and Coventry. It was originally an estate village accommodating workers employed at the fine mansion of Newbold Revel, which now houses the Prison Service training college. It is presumed that the settlement acquired its name from being close to the eastern lodge of the large estate.

There are only 40 dwellings, some of which cluster around a small green, and these include a magnificent listed long barn which gives access to one of the two farmsteads in the village. As there is no church, school, shop or post office, the focus of the community, other than the tiny village hall, is the Golden Lion Inn, which dates from the 17th century. An attractive gabled building raised up from the village street, it has been a popular meeting place for locals for many years, probably, at one time, dispensing ale brewed in the nearby brewery in the village, which is now a private house.

Unlike many freehouses today, the Golden Lion has been presided over by members of the same family since 1931. This continuity over the years has created a warm and friendly atmosphere throughout the character bars, and the food and personal supervision by the owners attract a loyal dining clientele from far and wide.

Low, oak-beamed ceilings, a few upright timbers, uneven part tiled and carpeted floors and an old inglenook with seating, characterise the charming main bar. Furnishings range from comfortable cushioned wall benches to darkwood tables and chairs, and there is a fine old carved settle. Numerous prints, brasses and jugs decorate the walls. A glass-encased section of wall confirms the age of the building. It shows wattle and daub from around 1620, with interlaced rods of wood and willow twigs plastered together with mud, clay and horsehair. A cosy restaurant area is adjacent.

On draught, one may find Flowers Original, Morland Old Masters and Theakston Best Bitter, served by handpump. Quality coffee is always on offer too. The busy bar food operation involves a help yourself system from a hot servery at lunchtimes and on Wednesday to Friday evenings, with a choice of four dishes. The regular printed menu offers a range of snacks – sandwiches, ploughman's lunches, vegetable pancakes – steaks and grills, lasagne, a seafood selection of dishes, as well as game and Guinness pie. Examples of the daily blackboard specials are herb and mushroom quiche, beef and vegetable pie and sliced pork in chasseur sauce. There is a choice of three roasts on the traditional Sunday carvery menu.

Children are made most welcome and under 12s have their own list of food. Extensive al fresco seating is available on the rear terrace and raised lawn, where you will also find a barbecue, a donkey and swings. The inn offers four spacious, well-equipped and individually-styled bedrooms, for those visitors wishing to explore the area further.

Opening hours: 11 am to 2.30 pm and 6 pm to 11 pm. Bar food is available from 12 noon to 2 pm and 6.30 pm (7pm on Sunday) to 10 pm.

Telephone: 01788 832265.

How to get there: Easenhall is 4 miles north-west of Rugby and is signposted off the B4112 between Rugby and Nuneaton. There is a large car park at the side of the pub.

Places of interest nearby: Coombe Abbey Country Park, off the B4027 near Coventry, H M Prison Services Museum at Newbold Revel College and the James Gilbert Rugby Football Museum at Rugby.

Berkswell
The Bear Inn

Despite its proximity to the sprawling conurbations of Birmingham and nearby Coventry (5 miles), this secluded and peaceful village retains much of its rural charm, with old timbered cottages, almshouses and farmsteads nestling around the village green, which preserves an unusual five-holed stocks. Recorded in the Domesday Book as 'Berchewelle', it takes its name from the shallow, 16 ft square well, located behind the almshouses and thought to be used in ancient times for baptism by immersion.

Completing the idyllic village scene is the splendid Norman church, which dates from 1150 and is probably one of the most interesting in the county, with its double crypt and a magnificent half-timbered room above its arcaded porch. It is surrounded by a beautifully maintained churchyard.

Just beyond the heart of the village you will find the Bear, which is often described as 'the perfect example of the old English inn', as it is a fine 16th-century timbered hostelry that was once part of Berkswell estate. In 1874 it was called the Bear and Ragged Staff Commercial Hotel, a name taken from the coat-of-arms of the Earls of

Warwick, who were once lords of the manor of Berkswell. Further evidence that the Bear had been an alehouse for many years can be found in the name of the equally impressive timbered building opposite. Called the Malthouse, it was formerly either a brewery for the pub or a storehouse for the ingredients.

The inn is believed to be linked with the period of the Civil War, when Cromwellian troops were stationed at Berkswell. During restoration a helmet and boot belonging to the era were found embedded in one of the interior walls. Further finds include two 1707 coins located under floorboards, and traces of earlier buildings.

On the terrace in front of the inn stands a Russian cannon, which was captured by Captain Eardley-Wilmot (lord of the manor during the 19th century) on 5th May 1855, during the Crimean War. It was brought back to the village and placed outside the Bear. To celebrate the occasion the gun was fired at one o'clock and a dinner held in the pub on 4th January 1859. It was fired only once again, to mark Queen Victoria's Diamond Jubilee, when, unfortunately, the blast shattered several windows in the village.

In recent years the inn has undergone significant modernisation, yet despite being 'opened up' and becoming a large commercial operation under the Chef and Brewer arm of the Whitbread Brewery, it still retains some fine original features. The oldest part of the building is the heavily beamed restaurant area, which was originally the kitchen and boasts two splendid fireplaces and an ancient 'head-cracking' central beam that came from nearby Cheylesmere House. Furnishings are neat and tidy and tasteful prints, plates and brasses adorn walls and shelves.

The long panelled bar dispenses Ruddles Best and County and Theakston Best Bitter, as well as a list of 21 wines. A hot food servery displays the 'Tavern' fare in the bar, which may include steak and kidney pie, lamb gypsy, lasagne, beef bourguignonne and vegetable and pasta bake. The restaurant choices are imaginative, with dishes ranging from whole lemon sole, medallions of pork tenderloin in cider and beef Wellington to rack of lamb roasted with rosemary and garlic. Also on offer are two and three-course set menus with a choice of starters and main courses, as well as Sunday lunches – plus a special price for under 10s.

A beamed upstairs room, known as the Cromwell Room and reached by an outside gallery staircase, is available for functions and meetings. Outside there is a sheltered rear lawn with picnic benches and a barbecue for summer use.

Opening hours: 11 am to 3 pm and 6 pm to 11 pm. Bar food is served from 12 noon to 2 pm and 6.30 pm to 10 pm.

Telephone: 01676 533202.

How to get there: Berkswell is signposted off the A452 between Kenilworth and Coleshill. There is an extensive car park to the rear of the inn.

Places of interest nearby: The National Exhibition Centre near Birmingham, close to junction 6 of the M42.

Berkswell Church.

8 Barston
The Bull's Head

The sleepy village of Barston lies on a broad hill encircled on three sides by the lazily meandering river Blythe. It was recorded in the Domesday Book as being isolated by the river, nestling among the marshes of Brodnock and Barston. The long main street is dotted with several 16th and 17th-century timber-framed cottages, the impressive Georgian-fronted Barston Hall and the attractive red-brick church of St Swithun, which was built in 1721 and altered in 1889. Just outside the village stands the splendid moated and timbered Eastcote Hall, built in 1669. Considering the close proximity of both Coventry and Birmingham, Barston is a secluded and unspoilt place.

Standing almost opposite the church is the homely Bull's Head, with its Gothic three-gabled, rendered façade. The unassuming outward appearance of this popular village local belies the true age of the property. In fact, it is a listed building dating back to 1490, boasting a timber-framed interior, which is clearly evident in the cosy rear dining room. The more recent and unusual frontage dates from the days when it was used as the village hall.

Further evidence of its age is the presence of a priest's hole, upstairs

23

in the private lounge area. The building is believed to have been an old malt barn before becoming an alehouse. In the 1700s the land in front of the pub was the main turnpike linking Coventry and Birmingham, and during this era the Bull's Head was a coaching inn, providing overnight accommodation and stabling for horses in the rear barns.

Today, it is a friendly, traditional country pub devoid of piped music and electronic games. The two simply furnished bars have a few exposed beams, small open fireplaces, various prints and plates adorning the walls and a comfortable mix of sturdy pub tables and chairs.

Owned by Mitchells and Butlers brewery (Bass), the pub serves their well-kept Brew XI, Bass and Tetley Bitter on handpump. The bar menu offers good value pub food. Familiar dishes on the printed list include rump steak, gammon and egg, home-made steak and kidney pie, lasagne and snacks, such as an interesting range of sandwiches with generous fillings, steakburgers and ploughman's lunches. A blackboard highlights the daily home-cooked items, for example, fresh tomato soup, prawn curry, cottage pie and, for dessert, bread and butter pudding and apple pie.

Summer al fresco drinking can be enjoyed in the delightfully sheltered side garden, complete with picnic benches. Children are welcome inside and out.

Opening hours: 11 am to 3 pm and 5.30 pm to 11 pm. Bar food is available from 12 noon to 2 pm and 7 pm to 8.30 pm on Monday to Saturday, except for Wednesday evening.

Telephone: 01675 442830.

How to get there: Barston is signposted off the A452 north of Balsall, 3 miles south of Hampton-in-Arden. There is a car park to the rear of the pub.

Places of interest nearby: To the south-west, two National Trust properties, Packwood House at Lapworth, and Baddesley Clinton. To the north, the National Exhibition Centre near Birmingham, adjacent to junction 6 of the M42.

Kenilworth
The Clarendon House Hotel

9

Kenilworth Castle, the finest and most extensive castle ruins in Britain, dominates the town and surrounding countryside. Originally a 12th-century wooden fortress, it rapidly gained importance, becoming a magnificent red-sandstone castle and a stronghold for the kings and nobles of England. John of Gaunt remodelled it as a palace in the 14th century and during the 16th century, John Dudley, the Earl of Leicester, enlarged the grand building, making it a place of lavish display and entertainment. It was Cromwell who ordered the castle to be demolished after the Civil War.

Beyond Castle Green, the attractive old High Street, lined with elegant 18th and 19th-century town houses, winds through the heart of Kenilworth's conservation area to reach the historic Clarendon House Hotel. The original timber-framed Castle Tavern was built in 1430 and the old oak tree, around which it was built, still supports the now much larger building.

The early prosperity of the tavern was due to the presence of a thriving market in the town, as well as its position on the old droving road from Balsall Common to Southam, and on the route linking

25

Kenilworth Castle to Coventry, which experienced its greatest activity during the Elizabethan era. During the 17th century, at the time of the seige of the castle, the tavern was reputedly used as the quarters for Cromwell's troops.

More recently the hotel has served as a horn comb factory during the 19th century, a builder's merchants and during the last war it was converted into flats. It was not until 1972 that the present owners acquired the premises and restored the building to its original use as a hotel. Although extended and refurbished, care has been taken to retain some of the original character with exposed old timbers, beams and oak panelling much in evidence in the comfortable Royalist Retreat bar and in the Cromwell's Bistro restaurant. The latter is housed in what was the kitchen to the old tavern and boasts a fine display of antique maps and Cromwellian armour.

The popular bar in this friendly freehouse dispenses Hook Norton Best Bitter, Boddingtons Bitter, Flowers IPA and Original and a regular guest beer on handpump, as well as an extensive wine list for diners to choose from. The printed bar menu features pub favourites, such as fish pie, chilli, chicken curry and substantial snacks like filled baguettes and jacket potatoes. The evening restaurant à la carte menu lists deep fried brie and avocado and prawns among the starters, followed by chicken Cromwell, pork and limes and fresh salmon with cucumber mayonnaise. Freshly-made puddings range from apple and strawberry pie and mango with red wine to ginger cream brûlée.

The hotel offers comfortable accommodation in 31 well appointed en suite bedrooms. Children are welcome in the restaurant.

Opening hours: 11.30 am to 2.30 pm (11 am to 3 pm on Saturdays) and 6 pm to 11 pm. Bar food is available from 12 noon to 2 pm Mondays to Saturdays. The restaurant is open 7 pm to 9.30 pm (to 10 pm on Fridays and Saturdays and 9 pm on Sundays).

Telephone: 01926 57668.

How to get there: Kenilworth is located on the A452, off the A46 between Warwick and Coventry. The Clarendon House Hotel is situated in the old town at the junction of the A452 and the A429 to Coventry. There is a car park at the rear.

Places of interest nearby: Kenilworth Castle, the National Agricultural Centre at Stoneleigh, Warwick Castle, Lord Leycester Hospital, St John's House, Warwick Dolls Museum, Warwickshire Museum at Warwick, and Leamington Spa, to the south.

10 Five Ways
The Case is Altered

A timeless atmosphere pervades this totally unassuming and untarnished 300 year old whitewashed cottage, which nestles beside a narrow lane off the A4141. Not only has this classic country pub resisted all modern-day intrusions, but it possesses an unusual name and a fascinating history.

Originally called 'The Case' after the lane on which it is located, the single bar alehouse occupied a cottage in a row of three dwellings, which included a bakery. During the 19th century, the then owner, the formidable character and matriarch Mercedes Griffiths, attempted to obtain a spirit licence, but her application was refused by local magistrates on the grounds that the pub was too small. Mercedes battled in her quest, eventually buying the adjacent cottage and bakery, thus increasing the size of the premises threefold. When the magistrates finally awarded her a full licence, the case was altered and the pub acquired a new name.

Mercedes presided over the hostelry well into old age, furnishing the delightfully unspoilt bars with various antiques and curios, a scene that has been lovingly preserved. The original bar is charmingly simple, featuring leather-covered settles and a mix of old pub tables and chairs on a red quarry-tiled floor. A brick fireplace with an open log fire warms the room on cold days and a couple of collectable brewery posters and a First World War Sopwith Pup propeller are the only decoration. The adjacent small bar is home to an ancient bar billiards table, which is still fed with pre-decimal sixpences. The old bakery now houses the splendidly old-fashioned lounge bar (open weekends only), which boasts a treasure trove of antique plates, china and carved oak furniture, as well as gleaming copper jugs and an open fireplace.

Real ales are drawn straight from casks racked on a stillage behind the main bar. Rare and unusual beer engines dispense the well-kept Flowers Original, Ansells Bitter and Mild and Sam Smith Old Brewery Bitter. On sunny days a pint can be enjoyed outside in the front brick-paved courtyard, beneath the chestnut tree, or in the small rear garden.

As with other traditional pubs that have been sheltered in a 'time capsule' for years, the provision of bar food is not a priority. The only solid sustenance available here is crisps and nuts, so plan your visit accordingly and come for the excellent ale and atmosphere, for this gem of a pub is a real rarity indeed. Long may it remain so.

Opening hours: 11.30 am to 2.30 pm and 6 pm to 11 pm.

Telephone: 01926 484206.

How to get there: Case Lane is situated just off Rowington Road, near the junction of the A4177 and A4141, 5 miles north of Warwick. There is a small car park to the rear of the pub.

Places of interest nearby: Packwood House (NT) at Lapworth, and Baddesley Clinton (NT), both to the north-west. Also Kenilworth Castle, to the east and the picturesque town of Warwick, to the south.

11 **Lowsonford**
The Fleur-de-Lys

In 1863, Lowsonford was known as 'Lonesomeford' after the isolated character of the village and the nearby ford which crosses a small stream. Although not large, the settlement is a scattered collection of some fine houses in the heart of an upmarket commuter-belt. Through its picturesque centre runs the fully restored Stratford-upon-Avon canal, at which point are located locks 30 and 31, a unique barrel-vaulted lock-keeper's cottage and the Fleur-de-Lys, an attractive canalside inn.

The draw of this attractive, long and low 17th-century pub is its tranquil village setting and the fine lawns which sweep down to the willow-fringed canal, complete with passing colourful narrowboats. It was originally a row of three charming cottages and an adjacent barn, which doubled as the village mortuary, with bodies awaiting carriage to nearby Rowington for burial. Conversion into a pub occurred over 100 years ago and the old barn now forms the galleried family room which, unsurprisingly, is reputed to be haunted. During the 1950s, a time when it was almost impossible to buy a meal in a pub, the Fleur-de-Lys was famous for its chicken and mushroom pies, cooked by the then owner, Mr Brookes, and attracting a loyal clientele from miles around.

Today, families seek out this atmospheric and friendly Whitbread Wayside Inn, as children are made most welcome and provision for them includes a special menu. The well equipped family room, complete with toy box and two rocking horses, is matched outside with a fenced-in playing area with excellent climbing frames. The picnic-bench filled, canalside lawn is a splendid and popular place for summer imbibing.

Within the pub, no less than six wintertime open fires warm a series of three rambling rooms, which boast low, heavily beamed ceilings, rug-strewn tiled and flagstoned floors and an assortment of old furnishings, including a carved oak dresser and large fireside chairs. Various prints, photographs and horsebrasses adorn the beams and walls. Magazines and newspapers are neatly arranged for your perusal.

Real ale drinkers will find the usual Whitbread-related ales – Flowers Original, Boddingtons Bitter – and a couple of guest brews, such as Morland Old Speckled Hen and Wadworth 6X, on handpump. The well-stocked bar also offers up to a dozen wines by the glass and a selection of malt whiskies.

Individual chalkboards arranged above a fireplace list the range of meals available. Changing options may include baked sardines, feta cheese, chive and tomato salad, home-made celery soup, aubergine pasta bake, chicken curry, venison pie or nut cutlets in a spicy bean sauce, followed by a selection of puddings. Meals are served with a choice of fresh vegetables or chips.

Opening hours: 11 am to 11 pm. Bar food is served from 12 noon to 3 pm (2 pm on Sundays) and 6 pm to 9.30 pm (7 pm to 9 pm on Sundays). Food is available right through the day – 12 noon to 9.30 pm – from Easter to September.

Telephone: 01564 782431.

How to get there: Lowsonford is signposted off the B4095 Henley-in-Arden to Warwick road, 1½ miles east of Henley. There is a large rear car park.

Places of interest nearby: All the boating and wildlife interest of the Stratford-upon-Avon canal is within easy reach. Two National Trust properties, Packwood House at Lapworth, and Baddesley Clinton, are to the north, and Hatton Country World (crafts and rare breeds) is to the east.

Henley-in-Arden
The White Swan Hotel

Henley-in-Arden, once set in the heart of the ancient Forest of Arden, is probably the finest small market town in Warwickshire, if not the country. Its broad, mile-long main street is lined with old oak-timbered houses and inns of every period of English architecture, from the 15th century onwards. Prior to this, the settlement belonged to Simon de Montfort, who owned the manor and the neighbouring parish of Beaudesert, but after he was killed at the battle of Evesham, Henley-in-Arden was razed to the ground. All that remains of the Norman castle built by the de Montforts is a hill called the Mount.

Among the significant buildings bordering the impressive High Street is the fine timbered Guildhall, dating from 1448, and two historic inns, in particular the White Swan which commands a central position. An inn has existed on the site since 1352, but the present timber-framed building is about 450 years old. During Georgian times it was the vogue to cover timbering, but during extensive renovation in 1935, the plaster was removed to reveal the original late 16th-century character of the inn.

In 1608 the White Swan was described as 'an inn with barns, stables, orchards and courtyard'. Many of these outbuildings were utilised to the full during the heyday of the inn, in the mid 19th century. It was a popular coaching house on the Birmingham to London route and 7 of the 22 coaches to leave Birmingham daily called here. From 1845 until 1903 the local court was held at the inn, and by the end of the last century it was one of 17 hostelries vying for trade on the High Street.

It is believed that Samuel Johnson wrote one of his books while staying here, and the inn was also a favourite destination for the poet William Shenstone during the 18th century. The ghost of an 18 year old girl called Virginia Black is said to haunt one of the upstairs rooms. She died after falling down the staircase during a quarrel with her lover in 1845.

The interior of the inn has been modernised over recent years, the main carpeted U-shaped bar featuring some original beams, traditional pub furniture and plenty of prints, books and bygones, creating a Victorian-style ambience. Across the courtyard is the part wooden and part flagstone floored public bar, which sports a collection of water jugs hanging on the beams and is the venue for live jazz on Wednesdays. There are ten letting bedrooms.

Owned by Ansells brewery, the inn serves four real ales, namely Tetley Bitter, Everards Tiger, Ansells Bitter and a regular guest beer. Conventional pub food is listed on a printed menu and includes filled jacket potatoes, various sandwiches, steak in ale, all day breakfast and stir-fry ginger chicken. Traditional roasts are offered on Sundays.

To the rear of the inn is a lawn with benches and swings, the town's bowling green until 15 years ago.

Opening hours: 11 am to 11 pm. Bar food is served from 11.30 am to 2.30 pm and 6.30 pm to 9.30 pm (7 pm to 9.15 pm on Sundays).

Telephone: 01564 792623.

How to get there: Henley-in-Arden is located on the A3400 between Stratford-upon-Avon and Solihull, 3 miles south of the M40, junction 16. There is a car park to the rear of the White Swan.

Places of interest nearby: Packwood House (NT) at Lapworth, to the north, and the Stratford-upon-Avon canal, reached to the east and south of Henley.

13 Warwick
The Ricochet Inn

Warwick is a charming walled town built on a low hill above the peacefully flowing river Avon, and dominated by the imposing walls and turrets of Warwick Castle, one of the finest medieval strongholds in Europe. Constructed in the 14th century on the site of a Norman castle, it was, until recently, inhabited for nearly 600 years by the Earls of Warwick.

The town suffered a disastrous fire in 1694, destroying 460 buildings, with only a few notable gabled and timber-framed dwellings escaping the blaze. Out of the ashes rose one of the most complete historic towns in the country, featuring a fascinating blend of architectural styles from every period over the last 700 years, especially some fine Georgian and Tudor houses.

Castle Street, as its name suggests, leads to the castle walls and one of the entrances to its attractive landscaped grounds. Although severely damaged in the Great Fire, Castle Street boasts one of the few surviving buildings, Oken's House, a magnificent Elizabethan timbered house that was once owned by Thomas Oken, a wealthy benefactor of the town. It now houses an interesting doll museum.

A short stroll along the street is the diminutive Ricochet Inn, a narrow two-storey Georgian-fronted building, squeezed between two larger dwellings. Built in the 18th century, its stone façade hides a splendid timber-framed structure, which is visible in what is now the restaurant. Deeds for the inn date back to 1722.

Originally called the Gold Cup Inn, it comprised just a tiny front room, making it the smallest pub in Warwickshire at the time. Recent refurbishment and sympathetic rear extensions have created a popular town centre bar and restaurant. Padded pine pews covered with attractive fabric in Jacobean design, matching drapes, round mahogany tables, a collection of horse-racing prints and an old pine-fronted bar, characterise the cosy and relaxed front room. Warm pine furnishings extend into the neat, rear dining room, which features a part red and black quarry-tiled floor, framed paintings and prints and an informal atmosphere.

Behind the minute bar of this freehouse one will find three real ales, namely Hook Norton Best Bitter, Wadworth 6X and a changing guest brew, such as Shepherd Neame Spitfire. The interesting list of 18 wines spans the globe and a blackboard highlights the two good-value weekly wine specials.

The imaginative handwritten menu changes every two months and will satisfy both those in need of a quick snack and diners wishing to linger over three courses. The varied starter or light meal options may include smoked salmon and scrambled eggs, grilled goat's cheese and bacon on a mixed leaf salad or whole smoked trout with a creamy horseradish mayonnaise and salad. Interesting main dishes range from home-made fishcakes with Hollandaise sauce, and fillet of sea bass baked with ginger, shallots and herbs to roasted breast of duck with a redcurrant glaze. Daily dishes chalked up on a board – medallions of pork with Stilton and bacon sauce, steak, ale and kidney pie – enhance the regular menu. Tempting freshly prepared puddings, such as chocolate mousse and traditional bread and butter pudding, appear on a separate list.

Children are welcome only at certain times, so please check first.

Opening hours: 11 am to 3 pm and 7 pm to 11 pm. Closed all day Sundays. Bar food is available from 12 noon to 2.30 pm and 7 pm to 9.30 pm.

Telephone: 01926 491232.

How to get there: Castle Street is situated off the High Street, opposite Church Street in the town centre. Turn right beside the Tourist Information Centre towards the castle and Doll Museum. The nearest car parks are along Castle Lane at the end of Castle Street.

Places of interest nearby: The castle, Doll Museum, St John's House, Lord Leycester Hospital, Warwickshire Museum, Yeomanry Museum, all in Warwick. Kenilworth Castle, to the north and the royal spa of Leamington are both worth exploring.

14 Warwick
The Tudor House Inn

Set beside the river Avon, this small and compact town is dominated by the majestic walls and turrets of Warwick Castle, built in the 14th century on the site of a Norman castle. With its fine medieval towers, dungeons, state apartments and beautiful Avonside gardens, it is one of the most impressive medieval strongholds in the country and until very recently it was inhabited by the Earls of Warwick.

Beyond the walls of the castle lie narrow streets lined with buildings from every architectural period during the past 700 years. Predominantly, the town is a pleasant blend of Georgian and Tudor styles with more modern infilling, as most of the splendid old timbered houses in the centre were destroyed in the Great Fire of 1694, which in five hours razed 460 buildings to the ground. The few that did survive include the magnificent timber-framed Lord Leycester's Hospital, which dates from the 12th century and was used as a guildhall from 1383 before being converted to almshouses in 1571.

An interesting survivor of the fire is the Tudor House Inn, which is an ornately framed, half-timbered building constructed in the early

17th century. Extensive restoration of this attractive three-storey inn has revealed the original timber façade of its elegant four bays. Each jettied floor boasts a different pattern of framing, the upper floors displaying moulded projecting floor joists and fragments of carving. The far right bay was probably added at a later date.

Black-painted beams and wall timbers characterise the interior, the long main bar featuring a huge fireplace at one end, an exposed section revealing the basic wattle and daub construction of the inn, and a small galleried area adorned with full sets of armour, helmets, pikes and other such items. Both bars and the adjacent restaurant are carpeted, furnished in traditional pub style and decorated with prints of local scenes.

Mitchells and Butlers Brew XI, John Smith's Bitter and Scrumpy Jack cider are available on handpump in this busy freehouse, which enjoys a good lunchtime business trade. A printed bar snack menu lists all the usual pub favourites, such as beef and mushroom casserole, lasagne and chicken curry, alongside freshly-filled rolls and ploughman's lunches. Highlights on the separate extensive evening menu include salmon and dill pie, fresh crab and mussel soup, roast quail Oriental, venison bourguignonne, various steaks and a range of five vegetarian dishes. There are daily chalkboard extras, like liver, sausage and black pudding casserole and lamb balti, plus Sunday roasts and a selection of puddings. A 'Hungry Hippo' menu delights the under 12s.

Outdoor eating is possible on a few front picnic benches close to the busy road. Overnight accommodation is available in eleven en suite bedrooms.

Opening hours: 11 am to 3 pm and 5.30 pm to 11 pm. Bar food is served from 12 noon to 3 pm and 6 pm (7 pm on Sundays) to 10.30 pm.

Telephone: 01926 495446.

How to get there: The inn is situated on West Street, south west of the town centre, opposite the main car park entrance to Warwick Castle. Limited parking at the front of the inn, otherwise park along West Street or in the castle car park (free).

Places of interest nearby: Lord Leycester's Hospital, the Doll Museum, the castle, St John's House and the Warwickshire Museum, all in Warwick. Kenilworth Castle, to the north and Leamington Spa, to the east.

15 Wootton Wawen
The Bulls Head Inn

Founded in AD 723 by Ethelric, who was given 20 hides of land by the King of Mercia to build a monastery, this may well be the oldest settlement in Warwickshire. Little more is known until about 1100 when a Benedictine abbey at Conches in Normandy established a small priory here, which was later bestowed by Henry VI in 1443 to King's College, Cambridge. From the mid-15th century the priory went into rapid decline and by 1840 little remained of the building. The earthworks visible in Church Field below the parish church are the only evidence of its existence.

Despite the modern-day intrusion of a busy through-road, Wootton Wawen is an attractive village, retaining much of its historic charm, notably the splendid white-stone church, established by Wagen. The church features almost every style of English architecture from Anglo-Danish up to the late Middle Ages. Not quite as ancient, but equally as impressive, are the graceful 17th-century hall and numerous timber-framed and whitewashed brick cottages, including the magnificent Bulls Head Inn. This charming, timber-framed building, with its clay-tiled roof, occupies a delightful position overlooking the church, and dates from 1597, when it was two substantial-sized cottages. Fortunately, it retains a lot of original character and appearance, despite various alterations over the years.

Prior to 1992, the Bulls Head was a Bass Toby Inn and since becoming a freehouse it has been smartened up and imaginative food has been introduced by the enthusiastic owners. Behind the wonky exterior walls lie three interconnecting lounge bar rooms, a restaurant and a separate taproom with a sawdust-covered floor, all of which are full of atmosphere. A wealth of low, heavy beams, wall and standing timbers, rug-strewn flagstones, old pine tables, pews and attractive co-ordinating fabrics characterise the comfortable eating areas.

The well-stocked bar dispenses six real ales – Morland Old Speckled Hen, Marston's Bitter and Pedigree, Wadworth 6X, Greene King Abbot Ale and Fuller's London Pride – and a regularly changing list of wines, including a good-value bin-end selection and several by the glass.

The emphasis on the interesting menu (served throughout the pub) tends towards fresh fish dishes, especially on the daily-updated blackboards, which may feature smoked fish salad and monkfish tails marinated in balsamic vinegar, tomatoes and fresh herbs. The regular menu meals include seafood tartlet and warm chicken liver salad, among the light snacks or starters, followed by salmon fishcakes, braised beef and vegetables, calves' liver and bacon and a seafood platter for two. Warm pear and cinnamon flan and creme brûlée appear on the pudding list.

There is a splendid sheltered rear terrace with a vine-covered pergola and a separate garden. Children under 14 are allowed in the dining room, garden and terrace only.

Opening hours: 12 noon to 3 pm and 6 pm to 11 pm. Bar food is served from 12 noon to 2.30 pm (3 pm on Sundays) and 7 pm to 10 pm (9.30 pm on Sundays).

Telephone: 01564 792511.

How to get there: Wootton Wawen lies on the A3400 north of Stratford-upon-Avon, 1 mile south of Henley-in-Arden. There is a good sized car park at the side of the inn.

Places of interest nearby: Coughton Court (NT), to the south-west, Mary Arden's House at Wilmcote, to the south and Henley-in-Arden. Wootton Wawen is also well placed for walks along the Stratford-upon-Avon canal.

16 **Southam**
The Old Mint

This magnificent medieval stone building looks rather incongruous standing as it does among its more modern neighbours on the main street. A series of fires during the 17th and 18th centuries, including a serious blaze in 1741, destroyed most of the ancient structures in this historic small town, which is an ideal base for touring Warwickshire.

Southam has long been an important settlement, as it developed on the major cattle and sheep droving road between Wales and London, and was granted a market in 1227. In the early 1830s the town became a noted coaching stop on the gruelling London to Birmingham route, with many inns needed to provide fresh horses and sustenance.

Of all the hostelries in the town at the time, the Old Mint, formerly known as the Horse and Jockey Inn, must have experienced the most illustrious past. Originally built as a monks' hospice in the 14th century, it acquired its present name after the battle of Edgehill in 1642. Legend has it that King Charles I stayed at the Manor House in the town and during his sojourn there he commanded the local noblemen to bring him their silver treasures, which he then had melted down at the inn and made into coins to pay his troops. The inn also minted Southam 'tokens' into the 18th century. These were a form of local currency in small denominations, the coin of the realm being too high in value for normal use. Only a few originals remain in existence in museums, but replicas are sold in the pub.

Beyond the mullion-windowed and rustic stone façade lie three restored bars with some original features dating back to the 16th century, including half-timbered walls, exposed stone and heavily-beamed ceilings. The atmosphere is enhanced by open log fires in winter, carved settles and an impressive array of weaponry, ranging from knives, powder flasks and antique guns to cutlasses and sabres, all housed in the popular Armoury Bar.

Generally this freehouse offers between seven and eight draught ales, the regular selection featuring Bass, Wadworth 6X, Hook Norton Best Bitter, Marston's Bitter and Pedigree, Timothy Taylors Landlord, plus two monthly-changing guest brews. In summer, cask cider is available and the bar also dispenses a good range of country wines.

The bar food is traditional pub fare, the printed menu listing steak and kidney pie, plaice and chips, curry, filled baguettes, ploughman's lunches and several vegetarian options. Examples of daily specials are beef and ale pie and chicken and mushroom pie. OAP lunches are a feature, and there is a children's menu. A good-value set lunch is available on Sundays.

To the rear is a sheltered terrace with picnic benches and a bouncy castle for active youngsters. Overnight accommodation is provided in two twin-bedded rooms.

Opening hours: 12 noon (11 am on market days) to 2.30 pm and 6.30 pm (6 pm on Fridays) to 11 pm, all day on Saturdays. Bar food is served from 12 noon to 2 pm (3 pm on Saturdays and 2.30 pm on Sundays) and 6 pm to 10 pm (7 pm to 9.30 pm on Sundays).

Telephone: 01926 812339.

How to get there: Southam is situated midway between Leamington Spa and Daventry. The Old Mint is on Coventry Street (the A423) in the town centre. There is limited parking to the rear, but a free car park is nearby.

Places of interest nearby: Napton-on-the-Hill, where the Grand Union and Oxford Canals meet, is just along the A425 to the east and is a good starting point for towpath walks. The Museum of Country Bygones at Marton and the Draycote Water Country Park are to the north of Southam, and Chesterton Windmill is to the west.

17 Napton-on-the-Hill
The Folly

The origins of the word Napton are Anglo-Saxon, meaning settlement (ton) on the top (knap) of the hill, and both Roman and Saxon relics have been found in the area. A settlement must have crowned this prominent 500 ft hill for a long time, possibly as far back as the Iron Age. Napton is now dominated by two landmarks, the predominantly 12th-century church of St Lawrence and the fully restored windmill which dates back to 1543. The village has long been of significant size. In the 14th century it possessed four manors, a weekly market and an annual three-day fair. Its continued prosperity and generally static population of 1,000 over the centuries has largely been due to successful agricultural practices, the construction of the Oxford Canal in 1790 and a once thriving brickworks.

As prosperity grew, so did the number of public houses needed to serve the workers, and by 1850 the village supported five pubs, two of which enjoyed busy canalside locations. With the Oxford and Grand Union Canals joining at Napton and providing the most direct route from Birmingham to London, the waterway was the centre of commercial activity in the village. The corn ground in the mill and the bricks and tiles produced in the brickworks were all shipped out of the village by horse-drawn boats, and villagers congregated by the canal to buy coal and other goods transported into the village.

The most popular meeting place for bargees, villagers and brickwork employees was the canalside Bull and Butcher (now the Folly), which was built as a pub 200 years ago. With its adjacent land it effectively became a smallholding or farm, serving ale and stabling the horses awaiting the loading of their boats. As the canal declined in importance with the arrival of the railway at the end of the. last century, the Bull and Butcher was the only canalside pub to survive, and it continued to do so until just after the Second World War, when traffic and trade on the canal virtually ceased.

After 44 years as a farm, this attractive brick building reopened as the Folly pub in 1990 to serve the needs of the flourishing longboat holiday business on the newly restored and rejuvenated Midlands canal system. The present owner still farms the 16 acres of land that surround the pub, keeping cattle and horses. However, the stables to the side of the pub, which once housed the bargees' horses, have now been converted into a canalware shop selling general provisions, ropes, fenders and brassware to modern-day canal users.

The traditional two-bar layout of the homely interior remains intact, the carpeted and wallpapered lounge featuring a large open fireplace, with an effective log fire in winter, and numerous rural artefacts – urns, lamps, pots and tools. Throughout the summer season, and at weekends all year round, the Folly bustles with activity, with both bars and the neat canalside garden, complete with children's play area and mini-museum of old agricultural equipment, full of towpath walkers, leisure boat users and local families out enjoying this splendid location.

Apart from its peaceful position, the attraction of the Folly is in the well-kept range of real ales on offer at this freehouse. Three regularly changing guest ales, such as Theakston XB, Younger No 3 and Home Bitter, accompany Hook Norton Best Bitter on handpump.

Its reputation is also spreading for the selection of home-cooked pies, which are served with freshly-cut chips. You can choose from turkey, wine and chestnut, lamb and mint, chicken, ham and mustard and traditional steak and kidney. Regular menu items include sandwiches, ploughman's lunches and ham, egg and chips, and occasional specials may feature pub favourites like chilli or lasagne. The Sunday roasts are popular and children's meals are always available.

Opening hours: 12 noon to 3 pm and 6 pm to 11 pm. Bar food is served from 12 noon to 2 pm and 6 pm to 9.30 pm.

Telephone: 01926 815185.

How to get there: Napton-on-the-Hill is located off the A425 Southam to Daventry road, 2½ miles east of Southam. The Folly is well signposted and has a car park.

Places of interest nearby: Draycote Water Country Park, near Rugby, and towpath walks along the Oxford Canal.

The Oxford Canal at Napton.

18 Aston Cantlow
The King's Head

Set deep in the heart of Shakespeare country, amid the charming lanes of the Alne valley, this historic village derives its name from the Norman family of de Cantelupe, who acquired the manor in 1205 and built a castle near the river Alne which, sadly, has long since vanished. Thomas Cantelupe, one of the early rectors of the parish, later became Chancellor of England and Bishop of Hereford and died in 1282 on his way to Rome to see the Pope. He was made a saint in 1320, the only Warwickshire rector to be honoured in this way.

The village comprises some fine old buildings nestling around a small green, including the magnificent early 16th-century Guild House, which boasts close-studded walls and a jettied upper floor. Now well restored and serving as the village hall, it is thought to have been the home of the Guild of St Mary, a religious association that provided priests for the church services.

Standing proudly opposite is the equally impressive, timber-framed and creeper-clad King's Head, which was once a pretty row of cottages. Flanked by a huge spreading chestnut tree and oozing old-world atmosphere, its main claim to fame is that John Shakespeare and

Mary Arden, the parents of William, supposedly held their wedding breakfast at the inn after their marriage in the beautiful 13th-century church of St John the Baptist in 1557. Whatever the validity of either of these events happening in the village – church register records did not begin until 1560 and the timber-framing of the King's Head may date from the 17th century – the story adds to the charm of the pub, which is a splendid destination for a pint or a meal.

Originally part of the local estate, and providing cider and ale to the estate workers, it was bought by Flowers Brewery in the late 19th century. Before 1984 the pub was run by a family related to the Ardens of nearby Wilmcote for 86 years.

The interior comprises two unspoilt, interconnecting rooms, boasting flagstone floors, a wealth of oak beams and a good mix of sturdy furniture including high-backed cushioned settles and old pine tables. There is plenty of gleaming brass everywhere, as well as old photographs of both the village and pub and a huge inglenook.

As this is a Whitbread tied house, Boddingtons Bitter and Mild, Marston's Pedigree, Fuggles Imperial and Scarlet Lady will be found on handpump. Value-for-money, traditional pub food appears on the simple, printed lunchtime menu, which offers such favourites as lasagne, home-made steak and kidney pie, breaded cod, ploughman's lunches and sandwiches. Evening additions include steak, ham salad, a daily curry and a vegetarian dish. More imaginative 'specials' are listed on a blackboard menu, for example bobotie, canneloni verdi, marinaded chicken and usually a Singaporean, Thai or Indonesian dish.

Outside, picnic benches adorn the peaceful side lawn. Children are made most welcome.

Opening hours: 11.30 am to 2.30 pm and 7 pm to 11 pm. Bar food is only available on Tuesday to Saturday from 12 noon to 1.45 pm and 7 pm to 9.30 pm.

Telephone: 01789 488244.

How to get there: Aston Cantlow is signposted off the A46, west of Stratford, and off the B4089 Wootton Wawen to Alcester road. There is a car park at the rear of the pub.

Places of interest nearby: Coughton Court (NT) at Coughton, Mary Arden's House at Wilmcote, Anne Hathaway's Cottage at Shottery, Ragley Hall at Alcester and, of course, Stratford itself, which is just 6 miles away.

19 **Harbury**
The Shakespeare

The 16th-century, part timber-framed Shakespeare inn is one of the oldest buildings in this substantial, bustling community, amid rolling farmland near the Roman Foss Way, which marks one of the parish boundaries. The history of Harbury pre-dates the Romans by far, as the place takes its name from an Iron Age noblewoman, called Hereburgh, who in 500 BC settled with her tribe on this hilltop position. Herberbury was probably a fortified camp and remains of a considerable earthwork can be located close to Harbury House on the eastern fringe of the village.

Harbury is, however, also associated with much earlier discoveries. In 1927 and 1928, at the now disused Lakin limestone quarry, workers unearthed two magnificent fossil skeletons of plesiosaurus and marine dinosaurs, and the latter can still be seen in the Natural History Museum in London. The earliest finds relating to human habitation have been in the form of Bronze Age cooking pots.

The Shakespeare is one of a number of hostelries serving the village, and although it is not the oldest pub, it certainly occupies the oldest building used as an inn. Located close to the now sail-less 18th-century windmill near the heart of the village, the Shakespeare was originally a farmhouse, the attractive half-timbered section of the building dating back some 500 years. It was not recorded as a public house until 1886 and over the succeeding years the pub has gradually incorporated the neighbouring cottages, the most westerly of which housed a dress shop as recently as 1969.

Despite recent alterations, the character of the old building has been retained, with original half-timbered walls and a wealth of beams and rustic stone in the charming opened-up dining area, which also boasts a huge central stone fireplace sporting good log fires in the winter. Additional dining space is located in the most recent addition, the light, airy and comfortable conservatory. The main bar area is more simply adorned, with the far room housing the pool table and games machine. A friendly and relaxed atmosphere prevails.

Owned by Whitbread, the pub dispenses a good range of real ales, namely Flowers IPA, Boddingtons Bitter, Timothy Taylor Landlord and a regular guest brew, such as Fullers London Pride. Diners will find the short, good-value list of wines of interest.

Highlights on the printed menu include substantial snacks – bacon batches with tomato, ploughman's lunches and sandwiches – with sardines in garlic butter and salmon mornay being among the choice of starters. Home-cooked main courses extend to steak and kidney pie, pan-fried salmon in white wine and prawn sauce with asparagus, pork in cider and rack of lamb. Extras on the daily specials board may feature fresh tomato soup, pork casserole and Mediterranean prawns.

Outside there is a delightful rear garden with picnic benches beneath a willow tree, an aviary and rabbits to keep restless youngsters amused. Children are also welcome inside.

Opening hours: 12 noon to 3 pm and 5.30 pm to 11 pm. Bar food is served from 12 noon to 2 pm and 7 pm to 10 pm, throughout the week.

Telephone: 01926 612357.

How to get there: Harbury is located 7 miles south-east of Leamington Spa, via the B4452 off the A425 Southam road. There is a car park to the rear of the inn.

Places of interest nearby: Chesterton Windmill and Ashorne Hall, to the west, the Heritage Motor Museum at Gaydon, to the south, and Leamington Spa Art Gallery and Museum.

Priors Marston
The Falcon Inn

Fine honey-coloured old stone houses with mullioned windows, built around 1650, congregate around the attractive 13th-century church of St Leonard in this peaceful and unspoilt village, which nestles on the lower slopes of Marston Hill. Commanding delightful views across the open countryside close to the Northamptonshire border, it has been described as being 'one of the most rewarding villages in this part of the country' and since 1972 it has enjoyed conservation area status, which should preserve the untarnished image that makes it a welcome place to visit.

The name Priors Marston originated from the Anglo-Saxon word 'merse' meaning marsh with 'ton' referring to town. The addition of Priors occurred in 1043 when the settlement was endowed to the Benedictine priory in Coventry by Earl Leofric. It may be difficult to imagine now but the village was once a thriving, bustling place, due to its situation on the Droitwich to Northampton Salt Road and the old livestock droving route between Wales and London. Later development and prosperity were aided by the presence of the Warwick to London coaching route, which passed through the village centre, and the close proximity of the Oxford Canal which opened in 1790.

One of the most striking stone buildings in the village is the Falcon Inn, built 400 years ago beside the old turnpike to serve passing travellers. Surprisingly, with the recent trend for unsympathetic modern pub extensions, it remains in its unspoilt, original form.

Although the interior has been modernised over the years, an ageless charm pervades throughout the single, rambling, L-shaped bar, which is spotlessly maintained. Delightfully free of present-day attractions such as piped music and electronic games, a cosy country ambience is created by the quality antique furnishings, tasteful prints, comfortable upholstered wall benches and settles, and the fine stone fireplace with its blazing log fire in winter. Exposed beams and stone walls enhance the atmosphere.

This welcoming freehouse offers a choice of four regularly-changing real ales, such as ABC Best Bitter, Burton Ale, Marston's Pedigree and Everards Old Original on handpump, plus a range of several malt whiskies and a couple of recommended wines of the week, in addition to the short, well-chosen list of wines.

The inn is a popular dining venue, as the range of home-cooked bar meals, especially the daily specials, are imaginative and well presented. Printed menu options include popular favourites, such as steak and kidney pie, chilli and a Falcon burger, alongside salmon steak, lemon chicken and a choice of four vegetarian dishes. The chalkboard menu may feature, for example, mushroom soup, lamb kebabs, beef in red wine and corn-fed poussin with bacon stuffing. There is a special Sunday lunch menu, and monthly 'theme' evenings.

Well-behaved children are welcome in the bar. Outside there is a pleasant rear patio for fine weather drinking.

Opening hours: 12 noon to 2.30 pm and 6.30 pm to 11 pm. Bar food is available from 12 noon to 2.30 pm and 6.30 pm to 10 pm.

Telephone: 01327 260562.

How to get there: Priors Marston, 5 miles south-east of Southam, is signposted off the A425 Southam to Daventry road. There is a car park at the rear of the pub.

Places of interest nearby: Napton-on-the-Hill, to the north, and a wealth of walks along the Oxford Canal.

21 **Priors Marston**
The Holly Bush Inn

This charming village lies on the lower slopes of Marston Hill in one of the lush rural areas of south Warwickshire. Fine views can be appreciated across the open countryside, with the Malvern Hills visible on a clear day. It was Pevsner who described Priors Marston as 'one of the most rewarding villages in this part of the country' and this was recognised officially in 1972 when it was designated a conservation area, in order to preserve its unspoilt image.

Like its neighbouring parish, Priors Hardwick, it was endowed to the Benedictine priory in Coventry by Earl Leofric in 1043, but its situation on the old droving route between Wales and London and the Droitwich to Northampton Salt Road aided early development. Later, the Warwick to London coaching route passed through the village and the Oxford Canal, built in 1790, is located on the fringe of the parish.

One of the oldest honey-coloured stone buildings that grace the attractive village centre is the Holly Bush Inn, which dates from the 15th century and is situated on a back lane near the predominantly 13th-century church. The recent discovery of a bread oven during renovations indicates that the inn was originally the village bakehouse. Beyond the ancient stone exterior are a variety of rambling rooms, some of them housed in neat and sympathetic extensions to the old building. Three winter log fires warm the welcoming, stone-walled bars, which are carpeted throughout and furnished with a comfortable mix of sturdy traditional pub tables and chairs.

The Holly Bush is a popular freehouse locally, offering on draught a range of real ales, such as Hook Norton Best Bitter, Bass, Wadworth 6X, Marston's Pedigree and Theakston Old Peculier. The pub snack menu lists, among others, ploughman's lunches, filled rolls, chicken tikka masala, chilli, salmon steak with herb butter, and ham, egg and chips. The comprehensive restaurant menu includes baked Brie, garlic mushrooms and home-made soup for starters, followed by noisettes of lamb with Madeira and mint sauce, sweet and sour duck breast, pork fillet with apple and cider sauce and prawn stir-fry Cantonese. Daily dishes are usually chalked up on a blackboard.

Children are welcome inside, where they have their own menu, and in summer the garden has swings and a bouncy castle to keep them amused. There are also hitching posts for those arriving on horseback. Overnight accommodation consists of four en suite bedrooms.

Opening hours: 12 noon to 3 pm and 5.30 pm (6 pm on Saturdays) to 11 pm. Bar food is served from 12 noon to 2 pm and 7 pm to 9.30 pm (10 pm on Fridays and Saturdays).

Telephone: 01327 260934.

How to get there: Priors Marston is located between the A425 and the A361, 5 miles south-east of Southam. Follow the 'Shuckburgh' sign in the village and turn right by the telephone box into Holly Bush Lane. There is a spacious side car park.

Places of interest nearby: Napton-on-the-Hill, to the north and a variety of walks along the Oxford Canal.

22 Alveston
The Ferry Inn

Separated by only a few fields from one of Britain's biggest tourist centres, Stratford-upon-Avon, picturesque Alveston clings perilously to its village identity. Absorbed into the borough of Stratford in 1924, the village is the older of the two parishes that comprise modern-day Stratford, and dates back to the Saxon period, when a settlement called 'Aenwulf's ton' was founded near the ford on the river Avon.

The parish, surprisingly, extends to Clopton Bridge in the heart of Stratford, but the unspoilt village centre clusters around a small green at the end of the lane leading to the Avon, 2 miles upstream. Old brick and timber-framed cottages and much larger walled properties give Alveston a secluded, countrified atmosphere, making it very desirable for Stratford-bound commuters. One famous resident, the author J.B. Priestley, lived for many years along the delightfully named Kissing Tree Lane.

Tucked among the attractive group of cottages facing the green is the Ferry Inn, an unassuming cream-painted pub that has become a popular destination with 'Shakespeare-weary' tourists wishing to escape the hustle and bustle of Stratford. To visitors unaware of the proximity of the inn to the river, hidden out of view along the adjacent track, the pub's name may seem rather unusual. It recalls the now defunct passenger ferry that once plied across the Avon, linking the village to Hampton Lucy on the opposite bank. Prior to 1910 the inn was called the Exchange Inn, but little is known about the age of the building, or how long it has been serving ale to the community.

The neat and uncluttered open-plan interior has a few original beams, comfortable, upholstered bench seating and open fireplaces, with a series of tasteful fish pictures adorning the otherwise plain walls.

Those who know come to this, consequently often busy, freehouse for the reliable selection of home-cooked bar meals. A large blackboard at the end of the bar lists the regularly-changing range of freshly prepared dishes, which are served in substantial portions. A starter, or snack, could be chicken liver pâté or avocado, crab and prawn salad, and among the main dishes you might find Hungarian beef goulash, Cantonese stir-fried chicken breast, rack of lamb, seafood pancakes or, maybe, stuffed aubergine au gratin. Examples of the mouth-watering puddings are rich chocolate torte and treacle sponge. There are also generously-filled rolls. As for drinks, you can choose from three ales, perhaps Theakston Best Bitter, Wadworth 6X or West Country Bitter, or opt for a bottle or glass of wine from the interesting list available.

There is a splendid front patio, overlooking the green, ideal for summer drinking. Children are welcome, but no under 5s are permitted in the bar.

Opening hours: 11 am to 2.30 pm and 6 pm to 11 pm. Bar food is available from 11.45 am to 2 pm and 6 pm to 9 pm (except Sunday evenings). Bookings cannot be taken, so arrive early to be sure of a table.

Telephone: 01789 269883.

How to get there: Alveston is signposted off the B4086 Stratford to Wellesbourne road. There is limited parking at the front of the inn, otherwise park along the village lane.

Places of interest nearby: 'Shakespeare's' Stratford and the Shire Horse Centre and Farm Park and Butterfly Farm. Also, Charlecote Park (NT), a couple of miles to the east of Alveston.

Priors Hardwick
The Butchers Arms

Priors Hardwick is an ancient monastic settlement situated just off the Welsh Road, the old cattle droving route that linked Anglesey with London. Hardwick was one of a group of villages given by the Earl Leofric in 1043 to the monastery he founded in Coventry. This village was destroyed at the time of the Dissolution and the site of the deserted village occupies a large grass field, known as Farm Close, behind the delightful little church of St Mary.

Development of the present village began in the 16th century, and its nucleus is the area close to the church and green, incorporating the magnificent mellow-stone building of the Butchers Arms. Built in 1562, the date inscribed on the chimney in one of the bars, this inn is very much the heart of the community and no doubt was a popular destination for weary drovers and travellers using the old Welsh Road.

Until 1973 the Butchers Arms was a humble, two-bar village pub catering for local needs. Since then the original building has been gradually extended and improved, with the sympathetic additions blending in well and enhancing the structure as a whole.

The pub attracts a discerning clientele from miles around for its charming and civilised ambience, and more especially for the food it offers, as the Butchers Arms could really be classed as a restaurant rather than a pub. Casual drinkers are provided for in the tiny panelled side bar, where keg Bass and Mitchells and Butlers Brew XI are dispensed. The splendid stone-flagged and heavy oak-beamed lounge bar is for enjoying pre-meal drinks and boasts a fine inglenook, which has a log fire blazing on cooler days. Quality floor rugs, upholstered wall benches, tasteful prints and lamps, gleaming copper and brass artefacts and a display of Civil War cannon balls found in the area, characterise this most welcoming of rooms. Expect to be greeted here by a smartly attired barman inquiring whether you are dining in the adjacent attractive, part-panelled and stone-walled restaurant. The toilets are first-class, too.

Those arriving in the evening for a bar snack will be disappointed, as lighter meals are only available at weekday lunchtimes, when one can choose from any of the starters on the restaurant menu. The extensive and varied restaurant menu presents a table d'hôte lunch and an à la carte dinner, featuring such dishes as grilled goat's cheese salad, smoked pork platter and mushroom and Stilton tartlet, for starters, followed by medallions of fillet steak au poivre, breast of chicken Wellington, roast guinea fowl in thyme and lemon sauce and a range of interesting fish dishes. Vegetarians are well catered for and all food is freshly prepared on the premises. Home-made desserts appear on a trolley. A set Sunday lunch is also available. To complement your meal there is an excellent list of some 200 wines.

Al fresco imbibing is a real treat here, and you can relax on the pretty flagstoned terrace, complete with gazebo, which overlooks the well-maintained, flower-filled garden. Children are welcome, but there are no reductions if they are dining!

Opening hours: 12 noon to 2 pm and 7 pm to 10.30 pm, when food is also served, but closed at lunchtime on Saturdays and on Sunday evenings.

Telephone: 01327 260504.

How to get there: Priors Hardwick is situated 15 miles south-east of Leamington Spa. Follow signs from the A425 at Napton. There is a large car park at the front of the pub.

Places of interest nearby: Historic Napton-on-the-Hill, and the Oxford Canal, which offers delightful walks.

24 Temple Grafton
The Blue Boar Inn

Temple Grafton, like most villages with 'Temple' in their names, is said to derive from the Knights Templars. The military religious order owned the estate in the 12th century and built the original church and fortified manor house. Prior to this, the land had been given to the Abbey of Evesham as early as AD 710 and later, in 1179, the manor was granted to Henry de Grafton, whose name survives in the village name today. Legend has it that William Shakespeare married Anne Hathaway in the original St Andrew's church in 1582, one of several villages locally to stake this claim. In 1862, the then lord of the manor, James Carlisle, demolished the church and manor, replacing them with the present church and timber-framed Court (not open to the public), which displays stained glass windows depicting scenes from Shakespeare's plays and Chaucer's *Canterbury Tales*.

Situated beside a crossroads, just east of the village centre, lies the creeper-clad, grey-stone Blue Boar Inn, which dates from the early 17th century and enjoys extensive views across the Avon valley towards the Cotswold Hills. Records indicate that it has always been an alehouse and individual landlords have been traced back to 1776.

Although modernised and extended over the years, the rambling series of rooms preserve the traditional charm and ambience of an old inn. There are part-flagged floors, some exposed stonework, numerous old beams and four open fireplaces. In the rear bar is a 35 ft deep, illuminated and glass-topped well, which is filled with pure water and is home to several large goldfish. Comfortable upholstered seating abounds, including two bay window seats that make the most of the view. To the rear there is a stripped-stone, walled restaurant with a selection of daily newspapers for awaiting diners to peruse.

This busy and efficiently-run freehouse is noted locally for its food and drink, the central bar servery stocking at least five real ales – Hook Norton Best Bitter, Donnington SBA, XXX and BB and Fuller's London Pride – and a choice of 50 different wines, including several half bottles. Most people come here to sample a home-cooked meal from the extensive menus. The bar snack list features filled jacket potatoes, sandwiches, chicken curry and seafood tagliatelle. More unusual fare appears on the restaurant menus (also served in the bar), such as poacher's hotpot, steak and kidney pie and lamb kidneys au poivre at lunchtime. Evening choices include duck and chicken liver pâté, fresh Cornish mackerel, peppered chicken, medallions of pork with garlic, onion tomato and herbs, and various steaks. Chocolate whisky pudding, crème brûlée and banana crunch may be among the freshly prepared desserts. There is also a Sunday lunch menu.

The flower-decked front patio with its countryside views offers delightful summertime seating. Children are welcome in the rear dining room.

Opening hours: 11 am to 2.30 pm and 6 pm to 11 pm. Bar food is available from 12 noon to 2 pm and 6.30 pm to 10 pm (7 pm to 9.30 pm on Sundays).

Telephone: 01789 750010.

How to get there: Temple Grafton is signposted off the B439 Stratford-upon-Avon to Evesham road, 3 miles west of Stratford-upon-Avon. There is a car park at the side of the pub.

Places of interest nearby: Ragley Hall and Kinwarton Dovecote (NT), near Alcester, Mary Arden's House and the Shakespeare Countryside Museum at Wilmcote, all the Shakespeare sites in Stratford, and the Scott of the Antarctic Memorial Window in Binton church, to the south-east of Temple Grafton.

25 Gaydon
The Gaydon Inn

The small village of Gaydon lies just off the B4100, between Banbury and Warwick, in the heart of arable farming countryside. The collection of buildings comprises some houses built with pale speckled bricks from the long-since-closed Gaydon brickworks, and a fine spired church, which, although it has an earlier ecclesiastical appearance and style, was in fact built in 1852 to replace an old chapel. Construction of the M40, thankfully just over a mile north-east of the village, and the reclassification of the A41 to a B class road, has enhanced the charm and peacefulness of the village.

The road which skirts the village has for centuries been a busy and important thoroughfare, well before the A41 carried motorway-volume levels of traffic. Back in the 18th century, in the days of rough dirt roads and stagecoach travel, it was a major turnpike linking Banbury with Warwick. Gaydon was an important midway destination point on this lonely, open road, as the only hostelry for many miles – the Gaydon Inn – was located here to refresh weary travellers and rest exhausted horses. The inn continues this tradition today, offering nourishment to local travellers, as well as tired and hungry M40 drivers escaping the rat-race at junction 12.

For 20 years at the end of the 18th century many lone travellers, coaches and tollgate houses on this stretch of road fell victim to a notorious gang of robbers from Culworth in neighbouring Northamptonshire, who terrorised this area. This band of a dozen men led by John Smith and his two sons, William and John, carefully planned their attacks, in particular at the time of the autumn fairs when people were returning with cash or horses from their day's trading. The gang's largest haul was £450 in gold from three unsuspecting farmers. After such raids the gang used to congregate at the Gaydon Inn to divide their spoils.

The activities of the Culworth Gang were finally given away by the drunken carelessness of some of the group. In 1787, John Smith and two others were hanged, but his sons were acquitted and set free. John Smith junior reverted to highway robbery, but exactly two years after his father's execution, he was arrested at a hold-up near the Gaydon Inn. After a night's imprisonment in one of the upper rooms, where he supposedly carved his initials and date on a beam, he was later hanged at Warwick. It is also certain that the famous Warwickshire highwayman, Tom Hatton, also frequented the Gaydon Inn before being caught at Warwick.

The inn has been much modernised to suit the car bound traveller since those notorious days of highwaymen. The pale yellow painted exterior hides three simply furnished and homely bars. The public, or 'Smiths', bar is the more spartan of the three and houses the juke box and games machines. Those seeking greater comfort should retreat to the woodblock-floored lounge bar with its red plush, padded wall benches, sturdy wooden tables and chairs and small, warming, wintertime open fire. Various horsebrasses, plates and plants adorn the walls and mock wall timbers in both the lounge and the adjacent rear dining area.

Owned by the Midlands brewery, Mitchells and Butlers (Bass), the inn serves Bass and M&B Brew XI on handpump, plus a regular guest beer, such as Timothy Taylor Landlord. An extensive and varied printed menu is highlighted by a good range of freshly prepared sandwiches, generously-filled jacket potatoes, steak and mushroom pie, shepherd's pie and at least ten varieties of the famous O'Hagen's sausages – real ale, venison, lamb and mint and hot Mexican, to name but a few. The home-cooked daily specials may include chicken and mushroom pie, corned beef pie, a curry or a freshly-made quiche. Vegetarians are well catered for too. There are also good value three-course evening meals and a choice of Sunday roasts.

Children are made most welcome and have their own menu from which to choose. There are a few picnic benches positioned along the front of the inn, but al fresco imbibers will have to be tolerant of cars rushing by.

Opening hours: 11 am to 3 pm and 5 pm to 11 pm, all day on Fridays and Saturdays. Bar food is available from 12 noon to 2 pm and 6 pm to 9.30 pm (7 pm to 8.30 pm on Sundays).

Telephone: 01926 640388.

How to get there: The inn is located beside the B4100, midway between Banbury and Warwick and only 1 mile from the M40, junction 12. There is a car park at the front.

Places of interest nearby: The Heritage Motor Centre at Gaydon and, further west, the Wellesbourne Wartime Museum and Watermill, and Charlecote Park (NT). The site of the battle of Edgehill is to the south and Burton Dassett Hills Country Park is the other side of the M40. Ashorne Hall and Chesterton Windmill are both to the north.

26 Stratford-upon-Avon
The Dirty Duck

Dedicated literature followers from all over the world make the pilgrimage to this historic market town because it was the birthplace of the celebrated poet and playwright, William Shakespeare, in 1564. Thousands of visitors every year trace his life from the half-timbered, 16th-century building where he was born, via the Grammar School he attended and the site of New Place (an Elizabethan knot garden) where he died in 1616, to the beautiful parish church beside the river Avon, where Shakespeare and some of his family are buried. The trail usually ends at a performance of the great man's work at the red-brick Royal Shakespeare Theatre, which was built in 1932 on the river bank and incorporates a museum and gallery.

Refreshment before or after the play, or even folllowing a visit to the gallery, must, traditionally, be taken at the Dirty Duck pub, which is located 300 yards along Waterside and enjoys an enviable position overlooking the attractive theatre gardens and the lazily flowing river Avon – an idyllic English scene. Once known as the Black Swan, it is the closest pub to the theatre and over the years has seen many stars of the stage, evidence of which is recorded in the panelled Theatre

Bar, which is festooned with signed photographs of visiting actors. Theatre-goers may rub shoulders with the famous after a performance or have fun putting names to the photographs on the walls.

The pub stands above and back from the road and comprises both numbers 53 and 54 Waterside. One of the cottages has a 19th-century, painted-brick façade hiding an earlier timber-framed building, the other dates from 1660 and is a stone-fronted, three-storey house. It was remodelled in 1738 with the addition of its handsome, yet odd, frontage.

There are two simply-furnished, beamed bars, each boasting much sought-after bay window seats which afford views across the peaceful river Avon to the recreation ground. The adjacent panelled restaurant is the setting for performance-goers to enjoy a relaxed meal before or after the play. A bust of the bard takes centre stage among the spirit bottles behind the spacious bar.

The 'theatre for gastronomic arts' menu served in the restaurant features home-made port and brandy pâté, smoked salmon and whitebait on the 'Prologue' list of dishes; highlights of 'Acts 1 and 2' include fish platter, roast beef and Yorkshire pudding, chicken Provence and steaks cooked 'as you like it'. House specialities range from smoked salmon and scrambled eggs, and braised oxtail to vegetable lasagne, while the 'all's well that ends well' pudding menu includes banana split and a traditional English pudding. The separate bar snack menu offers sandwiches, soup, ploughman's lunches and hot pies.

Fine weather imbibing can be savoured on the raised crazy-paved front terrace. Just along the road is the hand-operated chain-link ferry, which transports foot passengers across the Avon to the recreation ground and long-term car park – a useful short-cut!

Opening hours: 11 am to 11 pm. Bar food is available all day, and restaurant meals are served from 12 noon to 2 pm and 6 pm to after theatre supper.

Telephone: 01789 297312.

How to get there: Locate the bridge over the Avon and follow Waterside, passing the theatre to reach the pub. Limited parking is available along Waterside.

Places of interest nearby: Shakespeare's Birthplace, New Place/Nash's House, Hall's Croft, the World of Shakespeare, the Butterfly Farm and the National Teddy Bear Museum, all in Stratford.

Stratford is the 'Mecca' for literary enthusiasts dedicated to the life and works of the world's greatest poet and playwright, William Shakespeare. Each year thousands of visitors from the far corners of the world make the pilgrimage to this historic market town, intent on following the celebrated man's trail here and in nearby villages.

Despite its close links with Shakespeare, Stratford, fortunately, retains an identity of its own, with delightful watermeadows flanking the river Avon, a fine canal and architecturally exciting old buildings.

Few footsore tourists working their way between Shakespeare's Birthplace and the theatre will refrain from seeking refreshment in one of Stratford's most picturesque and ancient hostelries, the Garrick Inn. Tucked between a shop and the equally impressive Harvard House, the Garrick is a narrow and elaborately-timbered pub that was built in 1596 with Harvard House, after a great fire destroyed much of the town. Prior to this a building occupied the site from the early 14th century. The inn's striking timbered neighbour (open to the public) is worth a mention as it was the birthplace of Katherine Rogers, mother of John Harvard who founded Harvard University in America. These splendid jettied and gabled buildings are the most richly panelled and decorated in the town.

The Garrick has been an inn since 1718 and has had several names, including the Reindeer, the Greyhound and the New Inn, before acquiring its present name, which commemorates the Shakespearian actor David Garrick. He organised the Shakespeare Jubilee in the town in 1769 as a tribute to the playwright and this effectively established Stratford's future position as a major tourist attraction.

The present decorative timbered façade is not original. At the beginning of this century it was discovered that few of the surviving timbers were intact, so the front elevations had to be reconstructed, resulting in the ornate star-shaped panels. However, genuine wall and ceiling timbers grace the character interior, the cosy front bar possessing leaded windows, oak furniture, a rustic wooden floor and a small fireplace. A long, stone-flagged passageway leads to a larger, and busier, beamed dining room with a central copper-hooded fireplace.

Owned by Whitbread, the pub serves Boddingtons Bitter, Flowers IPA and Original on handpump and at least twelve wines are available by the glass. Individual chalkboards hooked on the wall beside the rear bar, list the food on offer. Dishes include steak and ale pie, cottage pie, liver, bacon and onions, lasagne and a late breakfast, as well as sandwiches and ploughman's lunches. Children are welcome in the dining area.

Opening hours: 11 am to 11 pm. Bar food is served from 12 noon to 8 pm.

Telephone: 01789 292186.

How to get there: Stratford is located on the A3400 between Banbury and Birmingham. The Garrick Inn is situated along the High Street, near Bell Court Precinct. Pay and display car parks are throughout the town.

Places of interest nearby: The Heritage Trail – the Shakespeare Centre and Birthplace, New Place/Nash's House and Hall's Croft – plus the Butterfly Farm, the National Teddy Bear Museum and the Shire Horse Centre and Farm Park. Mary Arden's House and the Shakespeare Countryside Museum at Wilmcote, Anne Hathaway's Cottage at Shottery and Charlecote Park (NT).

Anne Hathaway's Cottage.

28 Stratford-upon-Avon
The Shakespeare Hotel

Stratford-upon-Avon throngs each year with thousands of visitors from around the globe, because this small market town is famous for being the birthplace of the greatest poet and playwright that ever lived, William Shakespeare. In the town the 'Heritage Trail' incorporates the old timbered house in Henley Street in which Shakespeare was born in 1564, the Grammar School where he was educated and the site of New Place where the noted dramatist spent his latter years before his death in 1616.

Situated a few doors away from Nash's House along Chapel Street is the magnificent black and white, timbered and fine gabled façade of one of Stratford's historic inns, the Shakespeare Hotel. This striking, 120 ft long building dates back to at least 1637 and was originally three separate ones. The left-hand section of four gables formed two properties, which had to be rebuilt after an explosion damaged the Town Hall during the Civil War, and in 1764 the adjoining house became the original Shakespeare Inn and was one of the earliest exploitations of Stratford as the birthplace of the poet. Expansion of the inn, incorporating all four gables, occurred in 1778.

By 1814 the Shakespeare was rated highly in the town, as a coach house had been built to the rear of the inn, off Sheep Street. Improvements continued and its reputation grew, but it was not until 1880 that Charles Justins, an enterprising landlord who was aware that the Shakespeare connections were attracting more and more people to Stratford, leased the splendid adjoining, early 16th-century property, known as Five Gables. The Regency front and portico added to the façade in the early 19th century was removed and rebuilt in Elizabethan-style in 1920. Extended to the rear during the 1930s, the whole was then bought by Trusthouse Forte in 1946.

Having jostled with the crowds, you can escape from the throng of tourists and cars in the bustling town centre and relax in the Shakespeare's elegant bar and lounges. As one would expect, oak beams and timbers abound in the tastefully refurbished interior, which boasts period furnishings, deep sofas, attractive fabrics, quality prints and gleaming copper and brass, as well as open fireplaces with wintertime log fires.

Food is available all through the day. Enjoy sandwiches and pastries with coffee from the lounge menu between 9 am and 12 noon, the choice extending to traditional afternoon teas between 2 pm and 5.30 pm. Lunch and evening extras include additional sandwiches, home-made soup, pâté and various desserts. The timbered 'David Garrick' restaurant offers a set-price three-course menu featuring chicken liver terrine, basil and fish terrine and seafood salad among the starters. Main course options may include duck breast in cider sauce and best end of lamb with garlic crumble. There is an interesting global wine list too. A special pre-theatre menu is also available.

The hotel has 63 beautifully appointed bedrooms. Children are welcome throughout.

Opening hours: The inn is open from 9 am to 11 pm.

Telephone: 01789 294771.

How to get there: Stratford is located between Banbury and Birmingham. The Shakespeare Hotel is in the heart of the town, along Chapel Street. There is a car park at the rear of the hotel.

Places of interest nearby: The Shakespeare sites in the town, plus the Butterfly Farm and the National Teddy Bear Museum, and the Shire Horse Centre and Farm Park, a mile out of Stratford. Anne Hathaway's Cottage at Shottery, Mary Arden's House and the Shakespeare Countryside Museum at Wilmcote, and Charlecote Park (NT).

29 Broom
The Broom Tavern

'Beggarly Broom', as William Shakespeare referred to it, is an attractive small village comprising a pleasing mixture of historic and more modern buildings, located beside the river Arrow and close to Bidford-on-Avon, in which parish it lies. Scattered along three lanes, the community acquired its derogatory name through the activities of basket-making and knife-grinding and the pedalling of its products around the local markets. In an area rich in hard-working farming settlements, this way of living was considered exceedingly poor. However, strolling through the village today, it is hard to imagine how it could posibly have earned such a name.

Shakespeare was credited with a poem – or jingle – that appeared in a letter published in a magazine in 1794, and referred to eight villages to the west of Stratford, including 'Beggarly Broom'. Legend has it that the young poet wrote the poem after being involved in a drinking contest at the Falcon Inn in Bidford-on-Avon. Beaten by a team of men from nearby villages, Shakespeare and his friends began walking back to Stratford, but promptly fell asleep under a crab apple tree on a hill a mile out of Bidford. The story goes that, having woken up, the Bard recited the rhyme about the villages he could see from the hill. Others believe the jingle lists the eight villages in which he sampled the ales.

Whatever the truth is, the tale is an amusing one and is recorded on the inn sign that stands outside the ancient Broom Tavern on the main village street. Shakespeare is pictured asleep beneath the crab apple tree on the hill. The poet may well have quaffed an ale here as the charming brick and timbered inn dates from the 16th century, when it was built as a farmhouse, and is thought to be one of the oldest buildings in the village. In 1876 the premises comprised an inn and two cottages and were owned by Flowers Brewery.

Although modernised over the years, the interior still oozes charm and atmosphere, with heavy beams, and original wall timbers, especially in the cosy rear dining room. Upholstered wall benches, darkwood furniture and pictures of old Broom characterise the spacious main bar and the rear Shakespeare Bar.

The extensive printed menu offers a wide selection of dishes, including French onion soup, langoustines in garlic butter and smoked salmon mousse as starters, followed by pasta meals, omelettes, a choice of steaks, beef Stroganoff, lemon chicken and a range of home-made pies. Interesting ploughman's lunches and generously-filled French bread sandwiches are also available. Daily blackboard specials may include pork and leek sausages, spicy Italian meatballs, salmon, prawn and mushroom parcels and fresh fish dishes with various sauces. Traditional puddings are a feature, such as Bakewell tart or apple and sultana sponge. Regular theme evenings are very popular.

Three real ales are served, namely Theakston XB, Charles Wells Bombardier and a guest brew which changes every six weeks. Children are most welcome inside and smaller appetites are catered for. During the summer months a bouncy castle in the garden will help to keep them amused.

Opening hours: 11 am to 3 pm and 6.30 pm (6 pm on Friday and Saturday) to 11 pm. Bar food is served from 12 noon to 2 pm and 6.30 pm to 10 pm.

Telephone: 01789 773656.

How to get there: Broom is signposted off the A439 Stratford to Evesham road at Bidford-on-Avon. There is a car park at the pub.

Places of interest nearby: Kinwarton Dovecote (NT) and Ragley Hall, both near Alcester and Coughton Court (NT), a little further north.

30 Alderminster
The Bell Inn

Alderminster stands astride the busy A3400 in the heart of the picturesque Stour Valley, just south of Stratford-upon-Avon. Few travellers speeding through this generally unremarkable roadside settlement realise that the history of the village dates back to the 6th century, when a community of monks founded a convent here in AD 530. It later became part of Malmesbury Abbey, then a priory for Pershore Abbey 'for the maintenance of hospitality and infirm monks'. The present church, or 'minster', with its impressive lanceted central tower, dates from the early 12th century.

The village has long been associated with transport and communication. During the coaching era, Alderminster was a major stopping place on the London to Birmingham turnpike, and between 1826 and 1869 one of the earliest horse-drawn tramways, linking Moreton-in-Marsh with Stratford-upon-Avon, passed through the parish. The extra wide grass verge beside the main road indicates the line of the old tramway.

Built to serve the coaching trade, the Bell Inn thrived as a refreshment and resting stop on the long journey north. This tall, three-storied, Georgian building set hard by the A3400, continued to prosper, attracting car-bound travellers using what was once the busiest road to the Midlands, prior to the construction of the M40. In recent years the Bell has become a popular destination for discerning diners, as its bistro and bar serves some of the best pub food in Warwickshire.

More of a restaurant than your average village local, the much-refurbished interior is geared to dining, but the relaxed and informal atmosphere that pervades throughout the open-plan bar, dining room and attractive conservatory extension, is that of a pub. Immaculately maintained, the interior features a comfortable mix of tasteful furniture. Quality fabrics, wall and ceiling timbers, decent prints and an exposed brick fireplace with woodburner enhance the quiet ambience. The light and airy conservatory leads out onto a delightful rear terrace, complete with pretty oilcloth covered tables, chairs, tubs of flowers and a splendid view across the sheep-grazed fields and the Avon Valley – an ideal al fresco spot for a summer lunch or supper.

The kitchen prides itself on using fresh ingredients in preparing the extensive range of dishes that are listed on the imaginative, daily-changing blackboard menus. Typical starters may include cream of courgette soup, potted watercress and salmon, sweet and sour water chestnuts and mushroom and smoked haddock scallop, followed by minted lamb casserole, beef, kidney and oyster pie, calves' liver in a cream and herb sauce, rogan josh and rack of lamb with Madeira sauce. Fresh fish and seafood dishes are a speciality, such as turbot steak with watercress sauce, grilled lemon sole and fish and seafood casserole. Vegetables are good and well cooked, and interesting vegetarian options may feature hazelnut, brown rice and apricot roast. Round off your meal with one of the excellent puddings, for example, baked marbled chocolate cheesecake and peach and almond tart. Also available is a fixed-price, two-course weekday lunch menu and a diary of special themed evenings, ranging from symphony suppers to a Hallowe'en pie party.

Accompany your meal with one of the eight quality wines served by the glass, or choose a bottle from the comprehensive list available. The bar also dispenses three real ales, namely Marston's Pedigree, Fuller's London Pride and a guest beer, as well as an inventive selection of 'drivers' drinks. Children are welcome in the bars and smaller portions from the menu are provided.

Opening hours: 12 noon to 2.30 pm and 7 pm to 11 pm. Bar food is available from 12 noon to 2 pm and 7 pm to 9.30 pm (Sundays to 9 pm).

Telephone: 01789 450414.

How to get there: Alderminster lies on the A3400 between Stratford-upon-Avon and Shipston-on-Stour, 4 miles south of Stratford-upon-Avon. There is a large car park to the side of the pub.

Places of interest nearby: Charlecote Park, to the north-east of Stratford, and at Stratford itself, all the Shakespeare sites, the Butterfly Farm, Shire Horse Centre and Farm Park. Hidcote Manor (NT) and Kiftsgate Garden, near Ilmington are also worth a visit.

Edgehill
31 The Castle Inn

Edgehill is a magnificent beechtree-clad ridge that rises some 700 ft above the fertile 'Feldon' landscape of the Avon valley, affording extensive country views towards the distant Malvern Hills. At the foot of the ridge, just beyond the village of Radway, is the site of the first major battle of the Civil War, which took place in October 1642. King Charles I's army, marching from Nottingham towards London, was intercepted at the base of the escarpment by the Parliamentary army under the command of the Earl of Essex. The ensuing bloody conflict involved 30,000 men and by the end of the day it had claimed 3,000 lives.

Crowning the ridge, and making the most of the stunning vista, is the Castle Inn, which must rank among the most peculiar pubs in the country. Occupying part of an unusual octagonal, crenellated folly, also known as the Round Tower or Radway Tower, it stands close to the site where Charles I raised his standard to signal the start of the battle below. The mock castle was built as a gatehouse by local architect and squire Sanderson Miller between 1742 and 1749, to commemorate the centenary of the battle of Edgehill. He based his design on Guy's Tower in Warwick Castle, and locally quarried stone was used in its construction, with a wooden drawbridge linking the 70 ft tower with a smaller one.

The tower became an inn in 1822, when a descendant of Sanderson Miller sold it as a freehouse. Hook Norton Brewery purchased the premises a century later and have recently completed a major refurbishment of this bizarre building.

There are two homely, carpeted bars, the simply adorned public bar featuring an open log fire in winter. One wall of the fascinating and comfortable lounge bar boasts a fine mural of the fighting. There is also a display of Civil War memorabilia, such as replica pistols, swords, helmets and pieces of armour. Views across the battle site below can be enjoyed from the unusual arch-shaped windows, but the far-reaching panorama is best appreciated from the well-positioned side terrace.

The Castle Inn is a popular destination both for locals and for tourists on the Civil War trail, not just for its novel structure and unrivalled position, but for the highly regarded Hook Norton ales.

Traditional home-cooked pub meals are served in generous portions. Light bar meals include scampi, ploughman's lunches and sandwiches, and more substanial dishes, such as lasagne, mixed grill, pork casserole, gammon steak and steak and kidney pie, appear on both the main lunch and evening à la carte menus. Daily blackboard specials may feature chicken curry, home-made vegetable soup and pasta twists in tomato and mushroom sauce.

Children are well catered for. They are welcome in the bars, where they have their own menu, and the splendid garden has a play area.

Opening hours: 11.30 am to 2.30 pm and 6.30 pm to 11 pm. Bar food is served from 12 noon to 2 pm and 6.30 pm to 9 pm (9.30 pm on Saturdays).

Telephone: 01295 670255.

How to get there: Edgehill and the Castle Inn are signposted off the A422 Banbury to Stratford road, 6 miles north-west of Banbury. There is a car park opposite the pub.

Places of interest nearby: Farnborough Hall (NT), just off the A423 Banbury to Coventry road, and the site of the battle of Edgehill, within easy reach of the Castle Inn. Upton House (NT) is to the south and Burton Dassett Hills Country Park to the north.

32 Ratley
The Rose and Crown

Situated in a deep, sheltered hollow 600 ft up on the Edgehill escarpment, the yellow ochre, Hornton-stone village of Ratley is the highest settlement in Warwickshire and enjoys far-reaching views south across the Oxfordshire plateau. Fine old cottages, some of them thatched, jostle for position on the steep, horseshoe-shaped lanes that lead to the parish church and small green.

Just over a mile away is the site of one of the great engagements of the Civil War, the battle of Edgehill in 1642. As Ratley nestles among folds of hills high above the battle site, it was an obvious place for weary and wounded soldiers to retreat to during and after the battle, due to its hidden position. Many of those soldiers are buried in the churchyard, in a mass grave behind the church.

Located next to and closely linked with the church, is the 12th-century Rose and Crown inn, which was originally built as a cottage to house the stonemasons constructing the church. A listed building in the mellow golden stone that characterises the village, it is a simple and peaceful place and well worth escaping the beaten track for.

Until the early 1970s it was a very basic village local, comprising one room from which ale was served from a jug. Nowadays, although the single stone-walled bar is not much bigger, it is certainly more comfortable, being furnished with cushioned stools, window benches and darkwood tables and chairs, as well as boasting mullioned windows, an original central beam and a fine inglenook fireplace with an efficient woodburner. Sadly, however, the old, uneven flagstones have been carpeted over. Several prints, sketches and plates decorate the walls. The pub was enthusiastically rescued in 1992 after a two-year period of closure.

The bar is reputedly haunted by the ghost of a Roundhead, who hid in the chimney after fleeing the battle of Edgehill. Although he is friendly, various unexplained events have occurred in the pub and the landlady will willingly recount a few of these tales.

Being a freehouse, the Rose and Crown dispenses a range of ales, such as Hall and Woodhouse Tanglefoot, Charles Wells Eagle IPA, Bombardier and Fargo on handpump. The homely pub food attracts a loyal clientele, the printed menu featuring whitebait, Mexican tacos with spicy chicken, shepherd's pie, country lentil crumble, vegetable pasta bake, chicken tikka and cod and chips. Home-cooked specials highlighted on a blackboard may include beef goulash, curried kidneys, watercress and orange soup and a roast on Sundays. Children's meals are available at half-price.

Traditional pub games like chess, crib and dominoes are popular on dark winter evenings, while in the summer 'Aunt Sally' is played in the attractive and sheltered rear garden.

Opening hours: 12 noon to 3 pm and 6 pm to 11 pm. Bar food is served from 12 noon to 2.30 pm and 6 pm to 10 pm (7 pm to 9.30 pm on Sundays).

Telephone: 01295 678148.

How to get there: Ratley is signposted off the A422 Banbury to Stratford-upon-Avon road, 7 miles north-west of Banbury. There is a tiny rear car park for four cars at the pub, otherwise park along the village lane by a small green.

Places of interest nearby: Upton House (NT), just to the south, Farnborough Hall (NT), at Farnborough, the other side of the M40, and the site of the battle of Edgehill, north-west of Ratley.

33 Warmington
The Plough

Nestling well off the beaten track beneath the northern slopes of Edgehill, this is an enchanting, picture-book place. Rich, honey-coloured, Hornton-stone buildings encompass a spacious, sloping green complete with a pond and ducks. The winding village street climbs a steep, tree-clad slope, crowned by the ancient church of St Michael.

Well established at the time of the Domesday Book, the manor of Warmington was later given by the Earls of Warwick to the Benedictine monks of Preaux in Normandy. The village remained in monastic hands for some 450 years, the monks establishing a small priory here and supervising the building of the fine 12th-century church. Being so close to Edgehill, it is inevitable that Warmington will have associations with the Civil War. In October 1642, Charles I marched his army of 18,000 men through the village on his way to the first major engagement of the war. During and after the battle, soldiers sought refuge in the village and it is evident that several of them are buried in the yew-shaded churchyard, although the only marked grave is that of a Scottish captain, Alexander Gourdin.

Legend has it that during the battle three Roundheads hid up the chimney of the village pub, the creeper-clad, golden-ironstone Plough, which was built in 1604 on the hill between the green and the parish church. The story goes that two of the soldiers escaped, but the other died in the chimney and his ghost has haunted the pub ever since.

The Plough is a homely village local, its small open-plan, yet cosy, interior featuring a low ceiling with a heavy central beam, rough stone walls, a fine stone fireplace with a wintertime log fire and a comfortable mix of cushioned benches, settles and popular window seats, affording views down the attractive street. Old photographs, prints and brasses adorn the walls of the main bar and the more recent small rear extension. The friendly atmosphere is enhanced with traditional pub games, occasional live music and piped music in the bar.

After a stroll around this delightful village, the Plough is an ideal place to seek refreshment, for as a freehouse it offers three real ales, including the local brew, Hook Norton Best Bitter, Marston's Pedigree and a changing guest ale. There is a modest wine list and a range of malt whiskies.

Appetites can be satisfied with the generously-served bar meals, which include ploughman's lunches, sandwiches, ham, egg and chips, pâté, scampi, chilli and home-made cottage pie. Sunday lunchtime visitors can enjoy a traditional roast. Children are very welcome inside and have their own menu to select from. The little rear patio provides pleasant summer seating.

Opening hours: 12 noon to 3 pm and 6 pm to 11 pm. Bar food is served from 12 noon to 2 pm and 6.30 pm to 8.30 pm (except on Sunday evenings).

Telephone: 01295 690666.

How to get there: Warmington is signposted off the B4100 between Banbury and Warwick, 4 miles north of Banbury. There is a small car park to the rear of the pub.

Places of interest nearby: The site of the battle of Edgehill, to the west, Upton House (NT), to the south, Farnborough Hall (NT) to the east, and Burton Dassett Hills Country Park, to the north across the M40.

34 Whatcote
The Royal Oak

Situated in a tranquil spot amid narrow country lanes and a mere 5 miles from the Civil War battlefield at Edgehill, this sleepy historic hamlet boasts a mention in the Domesday Book, as well as links with the Parliamentary army. Despite some haphazard modern development, Whatcote is well worth seeking out, not only for its peaceful position, but for its fine, small, stone Norman church and the splendid Royal Oak pub, which dominates the village centre.

Built in 1168 as an alehouse for the workers constructing the church, this atmospheric, ivy-clad stone inn has a romantic history. During the 800 plus years that it has served ale, it is doubtful whether it has always been called the 'Royal Oak', as this pub name only became fashionable after Charles II hid himself in the Boscobel Oak.

A story surrounding this ancient building concerns the Civil War and the nearby battle of Edgehill. In 1642 the story goes that parliamentary troops, including Oliver Cromwell, used the pub as a temporary headquarters during the fighting and removed the bread oven to make an observation slit in the wall, to look out along the road towards the battlefield. Legend has it that Cromwell

81

and his followers returned to the inn after the fierce battle to slake their thirst and fill their bellies. A further reminder of its evocative past are the iron rings in the inglenook fireplace which lead up to a secret hiding place to the right of the chimney.

Throughout the long history of both pub and hamlet, the only real disturbance, other than the nearby fighting at Edgehill during the Civil War, to the peace and tranquillity of this hidden area, happened one night during the Second World War. A German bomber en route to a raid on Birmingham let loose eleven bombs over the village. Luckily, most exploded in adjacent fields, but one made a direct hit on the church roof, which was later expertly restored by local craftsmen.

The interior of the Royal Oak has altered over the years as the original mellow-stone building has been extended to cope with increased trade. The main bar oozes charm and character with its low beamed and boarded ceiling, old stone-mullioned windows, a huge inglenook with a small fireplace and seating and a mix of furnishings, from cushioned pews to a variety of chairs. The most recent extension houses the dining room. A miscellaneous array of curios, general farming memorabilia, old local photographs, brasses and a banknote collection adorn the thick walls.

The Royal Oak is a popular freehouse dispensing three real ales on handpump, usually Boddingtons Bitter, Bass and Marston's Pedigree. The bar food includes a selection of sound pub favourites on a printed scroll menu, from sandwiches and ploughman's lunches to seafood platter, chicken Kiev and sirloin steak. The blackboard list of daily specials may offer, for example, crispy vegetable pancakes, fresh local trout and home-made vegetable moussaka. Nursery puddings such as spotted dick and custard vie with apple pie, cheesecakes and gateaux.

Outside are the remains of the tree that gave the inn its name and the small side lawn with benches is a relaxing spot for enjoying an al fresco pint. Children are welcome in the eating area.

Opening hours: 11 am to 2.30 pm and 6 pm to 11 pm. Bar food is served from 12 noon to 2 pm and 7 pm to 10 pm.

Telephone: 01295 680319.

How to get there: Whatcote lies off the A422 Banbury to Ettington road, 4 miles north-east of Shipston-on-Stour. There is a spacious side car park.

Places of interest nearby: The site of the battle of Edgehill and Upton House (NT).

35 Ilmington
The Howard Arms

Located just beyond the northern edge of the Cotswolds, on the flanks of Ilmington Down, which at 845 ft is the highest point in Warwickshire, is picturesque Ilmington, one of the county's showpiece villages. A timeless gem, well worth exploring off the beaten track to find, as it bears all the typical Cotswold characteristics of mellow, stone-built cottages with mullioned windows, stone roofs and pretty, flower-filled gardens.

Spacious and neat, the collection of old cottages, a Norman church, a fine, gabled 16th-century manor and more recent dwellings surround two village greens – Upper and Lower Green.

Pride of place overlooking Lower Green is the rambling, golden-stone Howard Arms, a smartly kept village inn with a façade of five arched windows decked with hanging baskets, brimming with colourful flowers in summer. Obviously incorporating two striking buildings, the main bar area dates from the 15th and 16th centuries, when it formed two farmworkers' cottages. In 1780 a barn and stables were built next door and these were later added to the inn, creating the restaurant. The pub takes its name from one of England's most illustrious families, the Howards, who were tenants-in-chief of the village during the 19th century and who resided at Foxcote Manor, an impressive early-Georgian house with nine bays, located just south of Ilmington. The unusual, double-sided inn sign commemorates two events in the family history.

Period charm abounds in the well-maintained bar, which has splendid polished flagstoned floors covered with colourful rugs, heavy ceiling beams, exposed stone walls, two open fireplaces (one in a huge inglenook) and a mix of sturdy old and new pub furniture. Hunting and sporting prints decorate the walls and hopbines adorn the bar. There is a spacious, neatly-furnished restaurant and adjacent snug area.

The Howard Arms has a long tradition of providing quality food. The emphasis today is on good, home-cooked food, the daily-changing blackboard menu offering the same choices throughout the pub. Dishes may include celery and mushroom soup, and tossed salad with bacon and potato, for starters, with imaginative main course options, such as noisettes of venison with ginger and juniper sauce, hot poached salmon with basil cream, lamb and rosemary pie and rabbit and black pudding pie, all accompanied with fresh vegetables. There are puddings such as blackberry and apple pie or lemon tart to round off your meal. The bar stocks Everards Tiger, Boddingtons Bitter and Marston's Pedigree on handpump, and offers a list of reasonably-priced wines. Service is friendly and efficient.

To the rear of the inn is a pretty garden with fruit trees and flower borders, ideal for peaceful summer drinking. For a longer stay, comfortable accommodation is available in two en suite bedrooms. Well-behaved children are welcome in the bar and overnight.

Opening hours: 11 am to 2.30 pm and 6 pm to 11 pm. Bar food is available from 12 noon to 2 pm and 7 pm to 9 pm (9.30 pm on Fridays and Saturdays).

Telephone: 01608 682226.

How to get there: Ilmington is 4 miles west of the A3400 between Stratford and Shipston-on-Stour, 8 miles south of Stratford. There are car parks to the front and rear of the pub.

Places of interest nearby: Hidcote Manor (NT) and Kiftsgate Garden, both to the south-east. The Cotswolds are within easy reach, and Ilmington itself is set in excellent walking country.

36 Shipston-on-Stour
The White Bear Hotel

This attractive small country town developed during Saxon times around a ford on the river Stour and was originally known as 'Sheepwashton', or settlement-at-the-sheepwash. It soon became an important centre in the fertile pastoral area referred to as the 'Feldon', eventually gaining town status after Henry IV granted it the right to hold a market and a three-day fair. Shipston thrived due to its location on several major sheep-droving routes and became one of the greatest sheep markets in the country.

The town remained feudal until the construction of the London to Birmingham turnpike in 1730. This led to further expansion and the founding of some fine coaching inns, notably the George Hotel and the White Bear Hotel in the heart of the town. These provided refreshment to weary travellers and a change of horses for the coaches.

The White Bear dates in part from the 16th century and commands a prominent position overlooking what was once the market square. Originally of timber-framed construction, it suffered, along with most of the buildings on the east side of the square, severe fire damage after a serious blaze in the early 18th century. It was subsequently rebuilt with a Georgian brick façade and two attractive bay windows, yet the historic timbered structure is clearly visible in the well-maintained and characterful interior. In 1827, one of the rooms at the inn housed the town's theatre and it cost 2 shillings for a seat in the pits.

Upright timbers, part tiled and carpeted floors, sunny yellow-painted, rag-rolled walls, rustic scrubbed pine tables and high-backed oak settles, interesting prints and a warming wintertime log fire, all characterise the comfortable lounge bar. The cosy ambience extends into the rear terracotta-painted bistro with its checked tablecloths, fresh flowers and warm pine furniture. The more spartan public bar features a lovely old stone fireplace. A thoughtful touch is the selection of daily newspapers for customers to browse through.

Generally a bustling freehouse, especially at lunchtimes, the White Bear dispenses Mitchells and Butlers Brew XI, Bass and Marston's Pedigree on handpump. There is also an interesting choice of wines, including six by the glass and several bin-end bottles.

Bar food is of a high standard, all of it home-cooked using fresh local produce. As well as the unusual baguette menu, there is an imaginative array of daily dishes chalked up on a blackboard. This may highlight chicken and cider casserole, vegetable and lentil soup, venison sausages in red wine with red cabbage, and scrambled eggs with smoked salmon. Separate bistro menu choices include smoked kipper pâté, warm salad of bacon and Brie, and chicken, apple and cider pie, with chocolate and marshmallow mousse among the puddings.

A narrow staircase leads up to ten pine-furnished bedrooms, all with en suite facilities. Children are welcome in the bars and overnight. Outside, there are benches in the back yard and a small rear garden. Live music is occasionally featured.

Opening hours: 10 am to 3 pm and 6 pm to 11 pm, and all day on Saturdays. Bar food is available from 12 noon to 2.30 pm and 6.30 pm to 10 pm (except on Sunday evenings).

Telephone: 01608 661558.

How to get there: Shipston-on-Stour is located on the A3400 between Stratford and Oxford, 10 miles south of Stratford. There is ample parking at the rear of the hotel.

Places of interest nearby: Hidcote Manor Garden (NT) and Kiftsgate Garden, both north of Chipping Campden, Upton House (NT), northeast of Shipston, and the Rollright Stones and Long Compton, to the south, via the A3400.

37 Lower Brailes
The George Hotel

The attractive twin villages of Upper and Lower Brailes nestle on the flanks of Brailes Hill, the second highest point in Warwickshire, and command picturesque views across the rolling countryside of the Stour and Avon valleys. This unspoilt area of rich, open farming country is known as 'Feldon'.

The history of the parish dates back to before the Norman Conquest, when the manor of Brailes was held by a Saxon earl. After the Conquest, the land was retained by the Crown and by 1130 it had become one of the chief manors of the Earls of Warwick. The Domesday survey notes that Brailes comprised 46 hides of land, or eight square miles, the present area being around six miles.

In 1248 Brailes was granted a Monday market and soon became a thriving market town, the third largest in the county, attracting herdsmen and other traders from a wide area. By 1547 the town supported a population of 2,000. Early prosperity led to the construction of the beautiful church of St George, known as the 'Cathedral of Feldon' due to its majestic size. It dominates the local landscape and the charming old Cotswold stone buildings of Lower

Brailes, notably the splendid George Hotel which stands opposite the church.

It is believed that the present building was built in 1350 to house the stonemasons who constructed the church. However, it can be assumed that an alehouse was sited here a century earlier, providing refreshment for thirsty market traders, which gives rise to the claim that the George is one of the earliest licensed premises in Warwickshire. It was a celebrated hostelry during the coaching era, providing stabling, as well as having four acres of orchard and rich pasture in 1897. In 1920 the George Hotel was bought by the Hook Norton Brewery.

Subsequently, the celebrated status of the George declined, as happens now in many quiet, rural backwaters, and until only a few years ago it was in a near-derelict state of repair. Since then, new enthusiastic tenants and brewery investment have gradually transformed this fine building into one of the most civilised country inns in the area.

Beyond the flagstoned entrance lies the rustic-pine furnished public bar, boasting beams, a tiled floor and a huge stone fireplace. Across the corridor is the recently renovated dining room. The original charm and character of this part of the building has been carefully restored, with polished flagstones, huge oak beams, upright timbers and an enormous inglenook that was discovered in 1992, along with some old clay pipes and smokers' requisites. Scrubbed pine tables, baskets and bygones adorning beams, and tables topped with candles and flowers enhance the cosy ambience. To the rear of the inn, a panelled lounge bar leads out to a paved terrace and pretty garden, with rural views and a well-positioned children's play area.

Excellent Hook Norton Best Bitter and Old Hooky and a guest beer are dispensed on handpump and a list of 34 wines is available. Home-cooked bar food ranges from soup, pâté and ploughman's lunches to steak and kidney pie, lasagne and tagliatelle with creamy garlic and mushroom sauce. Daily specials may include chicken breast marinated in four citrus fruits and cold poached smoked salmon. There is a separate restaurant menu featuring pork Stroganoff, supreme of chicken and various imaginative daily dishes, all served with fresh vegetables. Home-made puddings complete the menu, and a traditional roast is on offer on Sundays.

Children are made most welcome in the bars and overnight in the two comfortable, pine furnished bedrooms.

Opening hours: 11.30 am to 3 pm and 6 pm to 11 pm. Bar food is served from 12 noon to 2.30 pm and 7 pm to 9.30 pm.

Telephone: 01608 685223.

How to get there: Lower Brailes is located on the B4035 Shipston-on-Stour to Banbury road, 3½ miles east of Shipston-on-Stour. There is adequate parking to the side of the inn.

Places of interest nearby: The Rollright Stones, near Long Compton, to the south, Broughton Castle, to the east, Upton House (NT), to the north, and, further north still, the site of the battle of Edgehill.

Broughton Castle.

38 Great Wolford
The Fox and Hounds

Great Wolford is a neat and compact collection of mellow Cotswold stone houses set in picturesque rolling countryside, close to the county border with Gloucestershire. Fortunately, the rural charm of the community has been well preserved since the Batsford estate sold the village in 1924, with only minor pockets of expansion and infilling altering the original character of the settlement. The village is partly enclosed by an ancient earthwork.

The peaceful village scene is enhanced by attractive cottages and fine gabled houses clustering around the small green, and by the splendid sharply-steepled 19th-century church of St Michael and All Angels, which commands unrivalled views across the valley towards neighbouring Little Wolford and beyond.

One of the oldest buildings in the village is the honey-coloured stone-built Fox and Hounds inn, which dates from the 17th century and features a timber-framed structure and leaded square-paned windows. It was built as a pub to serve the estate workers residing in the village and among the tales recounted over the years are those of a ghost and a secret tunnel to the church.

Like the relatively untouched village in which it stands, the Fox and Hounds remains delightfully unspoilt, its traditional interior exuding old-world charm. The cosy main bar and small adjoining dining room have polished flagstone floors, heavy black-painted ceiling beams – many adorned with jugs, or festooned with hops – an interesting collection of old furniture, namely high-backed cushioned settles, stripped pine tables and Victorian round tables. Pride of place in the bar goes to the fine inglenook fireplace, which boasts a log fire in winter and an old bread oven. There is a separate small tap room where time-honoured pub games can be played.

The enthusiastic owners maintain a well stocked bar in this established freehouse. Real ale connoisseurs can choose from a range of eight weekly-changing beers, such as Hook Norton Best Bitter, Smiles Best Bitter, Everards Tiger, Boddingtons Bitter, Shepherd Neame Spitfire or Greene King Abbot Ale. Non-beer drinkers can sample Bulmers Traditional cider on draught, one of an impressive collection of 130 malt whiskies, or select from a list of 22 wines, as well as several country fruit wines served by the glass.

Good home-cooked bar food ranges from a traditional printed menu selection, offering pork liver pâté, country-style soup, beef and mushrooms in beer, lasagne, chicken curry and peppered steak, to daily blackboard specials, such as chicken casserole, cheese and ham stuffed aubergines and game pie. Lighter snacks like sandwiches, ploughman's lunches and filled jacket potatoes are also available. Lemon cheesecake and sticky toffee pudding may appear on the dessert board.

A recent sympathetic extension has created three en suite letting bedrooms. Al fresco drinking can be enjoyed on the attractive front terrace, complete with flower borders and a covered well. Children are welcome in the dining area.

Opening hours: 12 noon to 3 pm and 6 pm to 11 pm. Bar food is available from 12 noon to 2.30 pm and from 7 pm to 9.30 pm.

Telephone: 01608 674220.

How to get there: Great Wolford is signposted off the A3400 between Shipston-on-Stour and Chipping Norton, 3 miles south of Shipston-on-Stour. There is limited parking at the front of the inn.

Places of interest nearby: Batsford Arboretum, Cotswold Falconry Centre and Sezincote Manor, are all located at Moreton-in-Marsh. To the south-east are the Rollright Stones, at Long Compton.

39 Long Compton
The Red Lion Hotel

Long Compton, as its name implies, straggles for over a mile along the busy A3400 amid delightful, rolling Cotswold-fringe countryside, close to the Oxfordshire border. Warm, mellow stone cottages of varying ages and styles line both sides of the road, with the unusual and handsome, thatched and timbered lychgate to the 13th-century parish church catching your eye as you drive past. Originally a cottage built in 1600, its ground floor rooms were removed to provide access to the church.

Until the late 19th century it was a local belief that witches resided in the village, with many a strange tale being associated with the mysterious Rollright Stones which stand at the top of Long Compton Hill, just south of the village. They are probably the best preserved collection of prehistoric stones in the Midlands and they attract many visitors to the area each year. Legend has it that this Bronze Age group of monoliths was once a king and his courtiers, who were turned to stone by a witch to thwart him becoming King of all England. The King's Stone stands apart from the circle known as the King's Men. Beyond stands another ring of stones, called the Whispering Knights.

Having gazed at the far-reaching views from the King's Stone and mused over the legends and evil deeds that surround the area, it is worth descending Long Compton Hill for refreshment in the homely confines of the Red Lion. Set beside the main road, this attractive, honey-coloured stone inn was built as a pub in the 16th century. The outbuildings were used for brewing and at the time of the coaching era the pub, with its adjoining stables, had become an important stop between Oxford and Stratford-upon-Avon. More recently, the stables and barns were incorporated into the pub and the old brewery equipment is prominently displayed in the bar.

Much of the original charm of the building has been retained throughout the four interconnecting rooms and separate dining area. Notable features include oak-beamed ceilings, exposed stone walls, some flagstone flooring, several open fireplaces and a comfortable mix of furnishings, from dark oak benches and a high-backed settle to traditional pub tables and chairs. Plates, china, old photographs and general farming bygones decorate the spacious interior.

The Red Lion is a freehouse dispensing Webster's Yorkshire Bitter, John Smith's Bitter and Morland Old Speckled Hen on draught, and a compact range of wines by the bottle and glass. The printed bar menu is a straightforward list of pub favourites, such as soup, sandwiches, lasagne, breaded cod and steaks. Blackboard specials may highlight dishes like dim-sum with hoisin sauce and grilled sardines with garlic. The restaurant's à la carte menu offers salmon steak Hollandaise and steak Diane among the standard choice of dishes. Puddings include apple flan and treacle tart.

Children are welcome in the bar, but on sunny days they can make use of the large side lawn. There is also a small patio near the road. Five en suite bedrooms are available for a longer stay.

Opening hours: 11 am to 2.30 pm and 6 pm to 11 pm. Bar food is available from 12 noon to 2 pm and 7 pm to 9 pm (9.30 pm on Fridays and Saturdays).

Telephone: 01608 684221.

How to get there: Long Compton is situated on the A3400 between Chipping Norton and Shipston-on-Stour. There is a car park at the inn.

Places of interest nearby: The Rollright Stones are, of course, a 'must'. Then, west of Moreton-in-Marsh, are Batsford Arboretum, the Cotswold Falconry Centre and Sezincote Manor. The high-up town of Chipping Norton, to the south, is well worth a visit.

⁴⁰ **Little Compton**
The Red Lion Inn

The tranquil parish of Little Compton is the most southerly in Warwickshire, tucked away in a secluded position amid rolling Cotswold countryside, a ¼ mile from the Gloucestershire border. Prior to 1845, when the county boundaries changed, the hamlet was in Gloucestershire and 2 miles away is the former Four Shires Stone, where the counties of Gloucestershire, Oxfordshire, Warwickshire and Worcestershire once met.

This is an idyllic English village, complete with charming scattered old cottages built of local stone, a green and a magnificent Elizabethan stone manor house, which partly encloses the walled churchyard. Remodelled in 1620, it was at that time owned by William Juxon, Bishop of London from 1633 to 1649 and close friend and confidant to King Charles I. Juxon was present at the king's execution in 1649 and a memorial window in the adjacent church of St Denis illustrates this.

The beautifully maintained garden, flower-filled in summer, of the friendly and civilised village inn, the Red Lion, is just the spot to appreciate the peace and quiet of this off-the-beaten-track village.

Built of mellow Cotswold stone, it dates back to the 16th century when it was a smallholding, the building only acquiring its licence in the 1890s. The pub's name is thought to originate from the fact that the village was located on the old sheep drovers' trail from Wales.

The homely interior comprises a simple public bar with exposed stone walls, a woodburning stove and various pub games, including a pool table. More comfort can be found in the unfussy, yet spacious, lounge which has a low, beamed ceiling, rustic-style furniture, some in neat cosy alcoves, and an open fireplace.

Visitors seek out the Red Lion for its honest and unassuming home-cooked bar food. The pub has a growing reputation for individually cut and cooked to order steaks, which are served with a choice of sauces. The largest steak ever eaten stands at 48 oz! Lighter bites on the printed menu include a range of favourites, from ploughman's lunches and filled rolls to ham, egg and chips. Interesting main course options include smoked salmon and prawn creole, marinated swordfish steak, seafood pie, steak and kidney pie and tagliatelle niçoise. Evening à la carte extras feature rack of lamb with redcurrant, port and orange sauce and fillet of salmon 'Duglere'. A traditional roast is available on Sundays.

One of Donnington Brewery's 15 tied pubs, the inn exclusively serves their BB and SBA beers on handpump, in addition to a well-chosen list of wines, including three by the glass.

Well-behaved children are welcome in the eating areas of the bars, while the more active youngsters can let off steam in the garden play area. With three comfortable bedrooms, the Red Lion makes a good base from which to explore the Cotswolds.

Opening hours: 11 am to 3 pm and 6 pm to 11 pm. Bar food is served from 12 noon to 2 pm (1.30 pm on Sundays) and 7 pm to 9 pm (9.30 pm on Saturdays).

Telephone: 01608 674397.

How to get there: Little Compton is located off the A44 between Moreton-in-Marsh and Chipping Norton, 4 miles north-west of Chipping Norton. There is a good-sized car park at the rear of the pub.

Places of interest nearby: The famous Rollright Stones, a little way to the east, Batsford Arboretum, the Cotswold Falconry Centre and Sezincote Manor, all west of Moreton-in-Marsh, and the attractive Cotswold town of Stow-on-the-Wold, south-west of Little Compton.